50 Tips for a Successful Job Search like...

Don't Wear White Socks To The Job Interview

JANICE M NIELSEN

 FriesenPress

One Printers Way
Altona, MB R0G 0B0
Canada

www.friesenpress.com

ISBN
978-1-03-918987-4 (Hardcover)
978-1-03-918986-7 (Paperback)
978-1-03-918988-1 (eBook)

1. BUSINESS & ECONOMICS, CAREERS, JOB HUNTING

Distributed to the trade by The Ingram Book Company

"Success is only a page away."
—Janice M Nielsen

TABLE OF CONTENTS

"Success has always needed a little help along the way!"
—Janice M Nielsen

FOREWORD

There are:
- Books on job search and career planning.
- Websites, templates, and apps for creating resumes and cover letters.
- Employment agencies and career coaches.

This book contains:
- Honest talk.
- Achievable steps.
- Responsible tasks.
- Tools for helping others.
- Support for parents, family, and friends.
- Help for employers.
- Some examples in story form.

Don't Wear White Socks to the Job Interview is a companion for the job search. There is something in this book for everyone. Keep it close.

REASON FOR THE BOOK

I decided to write this book after twenty years in the employment field. I am a Registered Vocational Rehabilitation Professional. I have given career assessments and used vocational assessment reports prepared by psychologists and occupational therapists to help individuals join the workforce or return to work. My work included providing workshops and training programs for job seekers. Some of the best learning came from the job seekers themselves. They did the hard work and shared their experience.

This book doesn't contain statistics or academic research. It contains proven job search life skills that work. I share what I have learned from my clients about their struggles to find employment. Most job seekers did not know where to start their job search. They didn't know what they were capable of or where they fit in. Some felt left behind. Some felt left out. Some were angry. Self-esteem and self-worth were pushed down by self-doubt. Sometimes, it was beaten down by guilt and shame. In extreme cases, anxiety was holding the person back. That first job would prove they could do whatever they chose.

It is inspiring to tell you that every person I worked with who was determined to find employment did! Many went on to rewarding careers. This book is designed to guide job seekers through the steps to get employment. The tips in these pages are based on honest, real-life examples for preparing in the best way possible. There were sincere and open discussions in group settings and my office. We talked about the hard stuff. They did the things that worked.

Please Note:
The opinions and advice in this book are mine. I have shared a few stories from my years of experience to help explain the tips. The names, places, and stories are fictional as they appear in the book.

YOU MATTER

Before you start this book, I want you to know that you matter. You are a gift to the world. There is only one of you. Your age, gender identity, culture, belief system, and unique abilities are all beautiful parts of what makes you who you are. You deserve the best life has to offer. Finding a great job is part of the journey.

When you get a job, your life will change. If you want to change your job or career, lots will change, too. Even thinking about that can feel scary. It can feel safer if things stay the same, but I want you to know that change happens. Even when we do nothing, change happens. Get ready to face change and move with it. Enjoy change. See change as your next adventure.

When you start looking for work, some days will be easy, and some days will be hard. When it is hard, it is easy to feel like giving up. I want you to remember that you have made it this far. You have this book! You can do this. You deserve a life of abundance, happiness, and fun.

Remember that life is all about choices. Your attitude and reactions are directly connected to what happens next. You can choose how to deal with things. When things happen that hurt, take some time away from the situation. Do something different for a bit. Go do something fun that makes you feel happy. Be kind and gentle with yourself. Then, go back and tackle the hard stuff.

Some people I worked with were mandated to take an employment program. This means they had to come and work with me. Many lived tough lives and had to cope with things like a lack of support and all sorts of abuse. I have only met three individuals who didn't want to work in more than twenty years of helping people find jobs. I don't know their reasons, and I didn't ask because they had a right to choose. I respected that.

Everybody else I met wanted a job or to return to work after time off. Some wondered how to start, where to look, or what to do. Others didn't think they could learn to work. Some thought no one would want them. Older workers assumed that employers wanted younger workers. None of that is true.

You matter. Go out and take your place in the world. Be ready for change. Believe in yourself. Get ready for work. Have fun!

GETTING STARTED

It isn't easy looking for a job. We must be brave and believe in ourselves. It takes courage and confidence.

This book is here to help:
1. Follow the tips.
2. Do the steps and exercises. Write in the book.
3. Learn about yourself. Improve your habits.
4. Set your goals.
5. Ask for help.
6. Take care of your reputation.
7. Share your success and challenges with someone you trust.
8. Don't stop until you get a job.
9. You matter. Never forget that!

Also…
It is about numbers. The more people you meet, the more resumes you put out, and the more interviews you have, the closer you get to a job.

STARTING THE JOB SEARCH JOURNEY

The following tips are about getting ready. They are about self-esteem and confidence. Paying attention to self-talk and beliefs that stop us from taking charge of our lives. Creating positive habits. Building a support system.

- Believing in yourself.
- Overcoming the fears.
- Taking the steps forward that need to be taken.
- Building your support system.

Personal development is valuable life-long work.

TIP №1
Believe in Yourself

Lee was shy and anxious. He was also bored and unhappy. Lee stayed home where he felt safe. Lee knew he was stuck. He wanted to do more and wished he was like his friends and family. They made it look so easy. They had jobs and money. They had friends and did stuff all the time. He wanted more but didn't think he could do what it took to get it. Lee didn't feel like he could push past his fear.

Lee needs to believe he is in control of his life.

You are in control of your life. Once you start believing this, you will see how to move forward. You will find the tools and support to help.

A job is a part of looking after yourself. Money is needed to do most things in this life.

"Yes, but…" It feels awful when things are hard, scary, or there is never enough.

These thoughts are how giving up or blaming takes over. This is how we get stuck.

Try this exercise.
1. Sit back and get comfortable.
2. Take a few deep breaths in and out slowly.
3. Close your eyes and think about something hard that happened in your life.
4. Continue to breathe in and out slowly.
5. Once you have that picture in your mind… think about how you got through that hard thing. Maybe you faced it or just waited until it passed.

6. Switch to thinking about now.
7. You are sitting and reading this book, following this exercise.
8. You are working on getting past a hard place. You are taking charge!

Lee was just stuck in a place he did not want to be.

Do you feel stuck? Read and then try the exercise below to help you get unstuck.
1. Close your eyes again.
2. Take a few deep breaths.
3. Picture some of the positive things in your life (small or big).
4. Think about the great things you have done.
5. Take time to remember just how amazing you are.
6. Now, imagine one positive thing you will do right away.
7. Open your eyes and write down what you will do.
8. Tape the piece of paper on the mirror in your bathroom.
9. Commit to doing what is on the paper as soon as possible.

Do this exercise often. Start believing in yourself right now.

Make a list of:
- Things you know how to do.
- Things you want to learn to do.

_____

_____

_____

_____

_____

What is one new thing you will learn how to do?

_____

_____

_____

_____

_____

MINI TIP

Things happen in life that will be out of your control. It is how you deal with those things that create your problems. And you are the only one who can fix things. Attitude, choice, and support are valuable tools to help you repair what needs to be fixed. Try changing how you deal with one thing this week and see if you notice a difference.

TIP №2
You Will Face Your Fears

Alex had a hard time talking to people. She would feel awkward and blush when she had to meet someone new. At school, she dreaded being called on to answer in class. Alex hated doing classroom presentations. They made her feel sick.

Alex tries to avoid groups and crowds. Most of the time, she stays home where she feels safe. However, Alex also wanted a job.

Fear is a normal feeling. We will often feel fear when we do something for the first time.

Shyness, low self-esteem, and lack of confidence show up as fear. Fear can make us avoid doing things. It can stop us from going after that job.

Here is what that fear might sound like:

"I want a job, but it is hard because I am shy about meeting new people."

"I want a job, but I feel uncomfortable around groups."

"I don't know how to talk to people, so I can't work in customer service."

"I want a job, but one where I don't have to work with others."

"I need to work in a space where no one bothers me."

Behind these statements is the fear of:
- Being out in the world alone.
- Meeting new people and not knowing what to say.
- Saying the wrong thing and being embarrassed.
- Believing that the same awkward situation will happen again.
- Being teased or bullied.

This all contributes to our fear.

F-false E-evidence A-appearing R-real = F.E.A.R.

We can talk ourselves into fearing anything and believe that we must stay away to be safe. Don't forget this! Fear stops us from trying because we are sure things will end badly. This holds us back from trying to get that job.

Fact

It is impossible to have a job and not interact with people. People with home offices have employers, supervisors, co-workers, and customers that they must talk with. They interact through the phone, online meetings, email, text, and video chats.

Remember

Fear creates a state of mind that allows us to make up stories about the future, treat them as facts, and believe they will happen. We believe that if it happens once, it will happen again.

Think about some of the fears you have about finding a job. Ask yourself if these fears keep you safe or hold you back. Be honest. If fear holds you back, work with someone you trust to get past them.

What we should fear the most is never doing new things!

What fear about working do you have?

_____

_____

_____

_____

_____

MINI TIP

Talk to people in your life about fears they may have. Ask them how they deal with them. You will see that everyone must deal with fear, and you will learn some ways to deal with yours. Who will you talk to first?

TIP №3
Yes, You Can!

Many people are very hard on themselves. Often, they don't even see it. If you are one of them, please stop being hard on yourself and start being kind and gentle to yourself.

Everyone has self-talk. Self-talk is the thoughts that run through our heads. We believe the chatter. Sometimes, it is positive.
"I make the best macaroni cheese."

There is also harmful self-talk. It is the mean stuff we say about ourselves.
"I am never going to be able to finish that because I am too slow."
"No one will hire me because I have never worked before."

Unfortunately, we believe this also. This is how we hurt ourselves.

We also do ourselves harm when we say things like we are:
• Too young.
• Too old.
• Too tall.
• Too short.
• Too slow.
• Too big.
• Too small.

Think about something you want and what is stopping you. Write down your hurtful self-talk and finish the sentences.
1. I can't because _____.

2. I shouldn't because _____.
3. I won't ever be able to because _____.
4. I don't have the money because _____.
5. I am not going to win because _____.

Now, go back to the sentences above and rewrite them using the positive self-talk below.
1. I can because_____.
2. I will because_____.
3. I will learn how by _____.
4. I will find a way to get the money because_____.
   (Maybe that first job will provide the cash.)
5. I am going to try because_____.

Don't forget that you are the first person who must believe in you! You can do whatever you choose to do!

What is the first negative thing you will stop saying about yourself?

_____

_____

_____

_____

MINI TIP
Write down things you want to do on a piece of paper. Tape it on the mirror in the bathroom, fridge in the kitchen, or wall in your bedroom. Focus on the positive. What you focus on, you will get more of!

TIP №4
Failures Are Part of Success

This tip is not about being reckless, causing harm, or making dangerous choices. It's about being brave enough to take chances and try new things. It is about going after what we want and being willing to fail as we go.

We can come up with lots of excuses to avoid failure. All excuses do is stop us from living our lives. What is going on is that we don't want to fail because we worry about what other people think about us. Here is a little secret. No one cares about our failures. They are too busy worrying about their own!

Being afraid of failure stops us from living our best life.

Fear of failure comes from:
- Low self-esteem.
- Lack of confidence.
- Feeling insecure.
- Feeling judged.
- Feeling shy.
- The need to be perfect.

Not allowing ourselves to fail means we miss out on all that life offers because all our focus is on feeling safe.

Being Safe is Not Living Your Best Life
Get excited about your failures. Failing means you are willing to take chances. You are not afraid of change. Failure is trying

new things and having new experiences. Failure is growth, and it brings you closer to what you want.

Being willing to fail means you:
- Take chances.
- Try new things.
- Have passion.
- Are motivated.
- Believe in yourself.
- Get more out of life.

Every failure has a valuable lesson. You learn new things every time you start over. Think about things that have been invented. How science works. How athletes are made. No one was born knowing how. We all must learn, take chances, and face failure. Failure is part of success.

People are far more interested and willing to help those who try and fail. Opportunity comes to those who put themselves out there. Employers look for people who are busy doing life.

What is one thing you learned to do because you never stopped trying? (Hint... if you can ride a bike, you failed a few times before pedalling away.)

Now, make a list of things you have learned by failing. Write down how you got past them.

_____

_____

_____

_____

_____

Give your failures a great big thank you! Talk about your failures. Write about them. Work on them. Be proud of them. Don't give up. Believe in yourself. Jump from try to the next, knowing you are closer to what you want after each one.

What will you do next that you have been putting off because you were afraid to fail?

MINI TIP

When we take a chance to learn something new, confidence grows. We start to get excited about life. Find something that interests you. Learn how to do it well. Fail and start again. Commit to becoming an expert. Keep a word or picture journal (or both). That is how we go from learner to teacher.

TIP №5
Your Support Team

Sandra was a very bright and capable young person who took a chance and joined one of my eight-week employment programs. Her self-esteem and confidence were so low that she could not see what she had to offer to an employer. Sandra lived with self-doubt and fear. Sandra had no one in her life telling her how awesome she was. Still, Sandra decided to leave her safe place and face her fears. By the end of the program, Sandra had friends, a support system, and a job! She was planning a career, too!

Surround yourself with people who believe in you and care about you. When you have love and support, your self-esteem and confidence will grow. You will start to believe in yourself and in what you can do.

Successful people don't get where they are alone. They have excellent support systems. Find support in your life. Support might come from family, friends, caregivers, teachers, or others. Be okay with accepting help when you need it.

Think about people in your life that you feel supported by.

Put their names in the following sentences:
1. I feel good about myself when I am around _____.
2. _____ points out to me when I have a negative attitude.
3. _____ believes in me when I tell them about my goals.
4. I feel safe talking to _____ when I feel stressed or fearful.
5. _____ calls me on my bad habits and self-sabotage behaviour.

6. _____ doesn't try to control me.
7. _____ makes time for me when I need them.
8. _____ offers me feedback and ideas when I ask.
9. _____ doesn't judge me.

Be Aware of Fake Support
It is valuable to look at the people in your life and decide if they are a support. Do the people in your life try to control you? Do they build you up or bring you down? Do they try to drag you into trouble with them? Do they support your goals?

There is toxic support. Watch out for people who always tell you what you want to hear. Be careful around people who are always doing things for you, even when they are not asked. These people often come across as the most supportive because they rarely want anything in return. They seem to put themselves last. It feels like they live for you and your success while ignoring their own needs and success. This is not healthy support! It is controlling behaviour that can lead to sabotage. Make sure you set good boundaries. Everyone appreciates something in return.

Give and Take
A real helping relationship involves giving and taking. Support systems work both ways.

Examples of give and take:
1. You might have a friend who is good at helping you practice for your job interview. Maybe you can bake them something.
2. A family member with several connections in the type of jobs you are interested in. In return for their support, you mow their lawn.

3. You have quit partying. Your friend joins you for a Saturday morning hike instead of the Friday night party. In return, you help them with their project.

4. You have a friend you can call on when you need advice, feedback, or to vent. They ask you to go with them to a community event, and you say yes.

That is how support works.

Remember

Different people will give different types of support. You don't need a fan club supporter. Choose someone confident and caring enough to tell you the truth.

Keep your support system healthy and cared for. Always return the help. Bake the cake or mow the lawn!

Who will you contact to ask for support to find a job?

_____

_____

_____

_____

MINI TIP

Self-care is an important choice. Be true to good sleep and healthy eating. Good friends are part of self-care. Balance your alone time and social time. Be grateful. Set healthy boundaries. Stay focused on your goals. Enjoy life every day. You are the one in control. What is one thing you will do today for self-care?

TIP №6
Practice Gratitude

A young man, I will call him Steven, joined one of my employment programs. He paid attention to all the learning. He was there to make changes in his life. Steven wanted a job and career.

On the day of his first job interview, Steven came to class dressed for success. He said he was ready. The team gave words of support and cheered as Steven left for his interview. Then we waited.

Steven didn't forget the workshop on gratitude. Before he had even returned to class, I got an unexpected phone. The call was from the employer that had just interviewed Steven. The employer was so impressed they had to call right away! This superstar showed up to the interview with a thank-you card and treats for the staff! The employer said this had never happened before. Steven got the job!

Each time someone helps you, they give you the gift of their time. Make sure you appreciate their kindness. Show that appreciation to teachers, trainers, mentors, parents, brothers and sisters, and other family and friends. Remember how valuable everyone is to your success. Tell people that!

Remember to say thank you when someone does something for you. Send a thank-you card or small gift when someone helps you with a resume or job interview. Cards and presents don't have to cost you a lot of money. They can be homemade or the gift of a little of your time. Decide how you want to show your gratitude based on each situation.

Some ways to express gratitude to others:
- Thank them in person. Tell them why you are grateful.
- Send a thank-you card or letter by mail.
- Share some of your time.
- Take them for coffee or buy them a coffee card.
- Offer to do some work for them around their house or yard.
- Pay it forward and mention the person who helped you.

Who will get your first thank you, and how will you thank them?

_____

_____

_____

_____

MINI TIP

Write down the name and contact information of the people who help you. This is valuable information. Store it for future reference. You might get a chance to thank them again later.

GETTING READY
Health-Grooming-Hygiene

The following tips are about appearance, health, and wellness. Paying attention to self-care so we start each day fresh, clean, and energized.

- Always care about your image and how others see you.
- Remember to make healthy choices to be sure you have the energy to work hard on your goals.
- Respect your body and look after it.
- Practice self-care every day.

We all benefit from a tune-up in this area from time to time.

TIP №7
First Impressions Count

Have you ever met someone and instantly liked them? Even before talking with them? Everyone has.

Have you ever met someone who you instantly didn't like? You don't know why. Some call it a bad vibe. There is just something about the person that turns you off.

We have all felt that, too!

You never get a second chance to make a first impression!

Did you know we judge people in the first three to five seconds of meeting them? Even before they speak, we are making up our minds about them. This is the subconscious mind at work, taking in information for us. The subconscious mind is part of our ability to protect ourselves. It is always at work. Our subconscious gives us those feelings about someone that we can't explain. It guides our choices and behaviour going forward. This is how first impressions work!

Good first impressions are essential when looking for a job. An employer's first impression of us might be part of the reason they hire or don't hire us. This means they may have decided about us in thirty seconds or less!

Once an employer has their first impression of us, they see us through that lens. They pay attention to what we say, what we wear, and how we act. They compare this to their first impression. Why? The most important thing about us to an employer is that we fit into their workplace.

First impressions are part of your public image. Yes! You have a public image! It is how you show up in the world. Pay attention to how others experience you. Don't leave anything to chance.

What You Wear

What impression do your clothes make? What do the words, pictures, and symbols on your shirts or hats say?

1. Do not wear clothing that could be offensive or discriminate against others.
2. By the way, that T-shirt with the beer logo or marijuana leaf does not belong on any journey to success. Save those for hanging out with the party crowd.
3. Always wear clean clothes that are not ripped or stained. Do not go to the grocery store in pyjama bottoms. Cover up your beach wear when you are not at the beach.

You never know who you run into when you are out and about in your community. You may bump into a manager who might interview you next week!

Tattoos and Piercings

Tattoos and piercings are part of today's culture.

1. Be sure your tattoos or piercings don't interfere with your success. Take some time to decide what to get and where to place them.
2. If you have piercings on your face, make sure piercings can be removed while at work.
3. Be ready to talk about your tattoos or piercings.

Swearing and Spitting

There are some poor behaviours and nasty habits. At the top of the list are swearing and spitting.

1. Swearing in public is something that people with low self-respect and self-esteem do. Swearing has absolutely no value in any situation. It ruins a person's public image instantly.
2. Spitting belongs in the privacy of a washroom where other bodily functions are looked after. It does not belong on the street. Spitting in public is so gross that it makes those who see someone spit feel sick to their stomachs. What is left on the sidewalk is disgusting.

Only you are responsible for your behaviour. Make the changes that you know you must make.

You Choose Who Is in Your Life
Another major part of your public image is the reputation of those you choose to spend time with. This includes friends and family.
1. The people you choose for your friends, the groups you join, and the people you spend time with say a lot about your values and beliefs.
2. If you are seen with people with bad reputations, others might assume you are just like them.
3. If the people you know are doing criminal things, then you won't be trusted. You will be seen as guilty because you spend time with them.

Manners
Don't forget manners. Manners are easy to use, so make them a habit. People won't forget how polite you are. If you don't use manners, people remember that!
1. Say please and thank you.
2. Hold the door.
3. Wait your turn.
4. Clean up after yourself.

Respect for Elders

If you are lucky to live a long life, you will one day be an elder. Think about how you would want to be treated when you are older. Treat elders the same way. Show care and respect.

1. Elders deserve to be treated with kindness, patience, and respect.
2. Don't dismiss their wisdom and value.
3. They also need help sometimes. Offer your support.

Remember

First impressions count! Everyone is watching and judging!

What is one change you will work on right now?

_____

_____

_____

_____

MINI TIP

Say or do something kind for someone every day. It will make their day. This will improve your mood and happiness, too! A winning combo.

TIP №8
Smile

Smile. Smile lots. You have a great smile!

We can smile anytime we choose. Have you ever thought about how powerful a smile is? Think about people you know who always have a smile on their faces. Think about people who don't smile. Which one do you like being around the most?

Did you know you can hear a smile on the phone? It is true. Try it! Answer calls with a smile on your face. It is almost impossible to sound angry, upset, or bored while smiling.

Smiling can change a mood. If you put a smile on your face, it becomes hard to stay frustrated or negative. Your brain starts to focus on good feelings.

Maybe you have perfected your smile for social media selfies. Now, it is time to share your smile every chance you get. Spread it around to others. Smile at people you don't know. You will be happily surprised when you get a smile back!

A well-timed smile might save a life. Think of the person walking down the sidewalk, head down, looking sad. They look up, and you smile at them. Your smile might be the message they were looking for. A sign that they matter and that life can and will get better.

Reasons to smile:
- Makes you feel happy.
- Shows people you are happy.
- Makes others feel happy.
- Makes you look younger.

- Makes you look good.
- Put you in a positive mood.
- Helps with stress.
- Makes other people want to be around you.
- Keeps negativity away.

Smiling is a **superpower**. Use it all the time. It works!

Where will you use your super smile first?

_____

_____

_____

_____

_____

MINI TIP

You can restart your day at any time. Stop and take a few deep breaths. Ask yourself if your bad mood is worth spoiling the rest of the day. Decide to get out of a bad mood. You can fix what needs to be fixed later. Sometimes, you won't need to fix anything. You only need some time away from it.

Choose to start your day over and choose to be positive.

TIP №9
Green Hair and
What YOU Wear

This tip does not include a person's natural hair or hair worn a certain way because of cultural and religious beliefs. There is no time, place, or excuse for discrimination!

Can you get a job with green hair? For many jobs, the answer is no. Neither will blue, pink, orange, or purple hair work. I have had many arguments with people of all ages about personal grooming. I have heard things like, "How dare employers take away my right to wear my hair the colour I want?" I agree, but I don't make the rules.

Everyone has a right to grow their hair, colour it, or shave it off. Where things get tricky is when you want a job. You need to pay attention to how you look. Part of that is your hair. Fair or not, you may have to tone down your style.

You need money to pay rent, buy food, and enjoy life. Why would you risk your ability to get a job so you can have "trendy" hair? Other people are looking for work who would lose their green hair to get that job. Think about it! Green hair or a paycheck? It doesn't seem like a hard choice.

Like it or not, employers can and will decide whom they hire to represent their business. Why? Employees are part of the company's image. Employers work hard to build their public image because it means business success. Looking your best is part of the image of the company. And you never know, after you prove yourself at work, the employer may be okay with some hair colour changes.

Haircare

- Keep your hair clean and styled. Wash your hair when it looks flat and feels greasy. A hat does not work.
- Get regular haircuts.
- If you have dandruff, use a good dandruff shampoo. If you have tried dandruff shampoo and it doesn't help, talk to a pharmacist or doctor about the condition. They can prescribe treatments for dandruff.

Beard and Mustache

- It is best to keep your face clean-shaven.
- If you do grow a beard, make sure it is kept trimmed short and clean. If your beard is patchy or peppered with grey hairs, it may look scruffy and get in the way of getting that job.

Clothing for a Professional Image

Showing our style is about what we wear. Sometimes, we choose clothes to wear in public that do not help our image. How did pyjama bottoms become a fashion for outside the house? We need to think about what our clothes say about us.

For your job search, follow the advice below:
- Logo-free T-shirts and hoodies.
- Pants that fit right and are not blue jeans.
- Suitable dresses and skirts.
- Clean, comfortable, and proper shoes that go with your look.
- Clean and ironed shirts and pants.
- Purses in good shape.
- Small packsacks that are free from stains and tears.

None of the things above need to be expensive. People with money shop in thrift stores! Ask someone for advice on what to wear. Put aside good clothes and shoes for your job search and interviews.

Keep clothes, coats, shoes, purses, and backpacks out of cigarette or marijuana smoke!

Express your style away from work. Stick to parties and clubs. Go out of town to rock your style!

What is the first thing you will buy for your job search?

_____

_____

_____

_____

MINI TIP

Everyone has things about themselves that they would love to change. It doesn't matter who you are. Don't compare yourself to others. Don't compare yourself to what you see online. And remember, you will never be any younger than you are today.

Start a list of all the things that are awesome about you. Put the list on your fridge or bedroom door. Add to it often. Then get going and enjoy life right now!

TIP №10
Up Close and Personal

Personal hygiene is about being clean and smelling fresh. It involves the whole body. Most personal hygiene is a habit. Good habits work, but sometimes people forget or speed through. For example, some neglect to brush and floss their teeth or get lazy. A checklist is a great way to stay on track with a hygiene routine.

Taking care of our body is a part of wellness and living a healthy, positive life. When we are healthy, we can achieve our goals.

Checklist:

Sleep Hygiene
Sleep is part of health and wellness. Our body heals and repairs itself when we sleep. Waking up tired every day makes life hard. Some people sabotage their sleep with habits that they can change. For example, gaming or scrolling social media before bedtime hurts our sleep.

For people who do their best to get a good night's rest and can't because of worry or stress, please talk to a nurse or a doctor. They will help you.

Teeth and Breath
Brush your teeth at least three times a day. Floss before bedtime or more often. Carry a toothbrush and toothpaste with you. Make sure your breath is fresh. Carry breath spray, breath strips,

or mints. Avoid gum. One business owner told me they will not hire someone who chews gum!

Did you know the white or yellow stuff along the gum line that doesn't come off with brushing has a name? It is called *dental calculus*. It is on the teeth when teeth are not brushed and flossed enough. This stuff smells very bad. It is a build-up of old food. The good news is that it can be removed by a dental hygienist when they clean the teeth.

Remember: some jobs come with dental benefits, so you might have regular dental care once you are working.

Skin

A shower or bath starts the day off right. Warm, soapy water gives us a fresh start to the day. There are over-the-counter face washes and creams for oily or dry skin. Talk to a doctor if you have acne that is causing you stress. There is help available.

Hand Washing and Fingernails

Don't forget to wash your hands regularly throughout the day. Hand washing helps prevent illness.

Clean your fingernails and cut them regularly. If you wear nail polish, choose light and remove chipped polish immediately. You cannot have long or artificial nails if you work with food. They are not hygienic.

Foot Health

Many jobs require standing for hours. This can cause sore feet. Soak sore, tired feet. Get good-fitting shoes with support. In some workplaces, you will need safety shoes.

Keep feet clean and dry. Wear socks made from cotton. Standing all day can cause sweaty feet. Foot odour happens when feet sweat. Check shoes for odour. If they smell, throw them out and get new shoes. If you have any concerns, see a doctor. You might have a foot condition and need attention.

Body Odour

Armpit body odour is a fact of life. Cleaning underarms with a good soap and use an unscented deodorant. Some people must wash their armpits a few times a day. If the odour is a real problem, talk to a pharmacist or a doctor. There are products and treatments available. Do not try to mask body odour with scented products. It just makes the smell worse.

Smoking

Do not smoke before an interview. The smell will be in your hair and on your skin. Your interview clothes will smell. Don't fool yourself that mints will cover up the nasty breath. Non-smokers will smell that cigarette!

Did you know that many employers will choose a non-smoker over a smoker if both job seekers are equal? Why? Less sick time and fewer break times.

Remember, even on the rough days when you feel like staying in bed under the covers, if you get up, shower, and get dressed, you start to feel more positive and in control of your day.

What is one thing you will improve or change today?

_____

_____

_____

_____

_____

_____

MINI TIP

Even as an individual, you can make a difference in positive ways. Your shopping choices are one way to help with positive change. When you buy grooming products made with healthy ingredients, not tested on animals and are not harmful to the environment, you are helping yourself, others, animals, and the planet. Pick one of the products you use today and do some internet research on it. See what ingredients it contains and if it is cruelty-free. Maybe there is a better product out there.

TIP №11
Substance Use and Abuse

If you are struggling with drug or alcohol abuse, please get help now! You deserve it!

Substance Use
The most important thing to know about using alcohol and drugs is that they are poison. The poison starts to destroy the body right away. It may feel harmless in the beginning, but abusing alcohol and marijuana, using street drugs, or abusing prescription drugs leads to problems. Substance abuse harms the body, mind, and life very quickly.

Clear signs there is a problem:
- Using alcohol to have fun.
- Blacking out when drinking.
- Smoking marijuana throughout the day.
- Sleeping most of the day.
- Lying about substance use.
- Needing to use alcohol or drugs to feel better.
- Spending money on alcohol or drugs instead of food or bills.
- Losing relationships with family and close friends.
- Hanging out with other drug users.
- Feeling scared and stuck.
- Low motivation.
- Lack of joy and inspiration.
- Low self-esteem and secret self-dislike.
- Blaming others for the situation and problems.

Substance Use and Work

People who abuse alcohol or drugs miss work. Some people come to work with alcohol or drugs still in their bodies. Substance abuse makes the workplace unsafe and is a serious cause of accidents and loss of production.

Substance abuse issues hurt the company. It costs employers money that they shouldn't have to spend. For example, when an employee calls in sick, someone must replace them for the day. If there is no one to come to work, then the business is short of workers. The situation is difficult for the other staff, customers, and the company. If the employee misses too much work, the employer will replace them with a more reliable employee.

Employers cannot afford to keep an employee who uses alcohol or drugs unless the employee commits to getting help and then gets the help they need.

Employment Probation Period

Employment probationary periods are part of employment law. Probation is the time that employers use to determine if the new person is a good fit for the job. A probationary period is usually 3-6 months. An employer can dismiss a new employee during the probationary period without a reason. Employers may have a probationary period for new employees in their hiring contract. Find out the probationary period for the job you are interested in.

Substance abuse shows up very quickly. Alcohol and drug abuse ruin jobs and careers.

If you struggle with substance abuse, please get help. You are not alone. There is support for those who want it. It is never too late to get clean and sober. Abusing drugs or alcohol never gets better. It always gets worse. It robs you of your health, family, friends, finances, goals, values, and life. It can lead to overdose and death.

There are many success stories about people who have come back from addiction. They found support for managing their trauma that didn't harm them further. They have taken their life back. Be one of them!

Do you, or someone you know, need some support around substance abuse? What will you do?

_____

_____

_____

_____

_____

MINI TIP

There are so many healthy ways to get excited about life. Get a hobby. Make art, learn to cook, do sports, travel, help others, or invent something. Join groups that interest you. Study something and become an expert on it. It doesn't have to cost in the beginning. Fill that empty part of you with healthy choices, not harmful ones. What is one thing you would like to learn?

TIP №12
Wear Black Socks

I tell every job seeker to wear black socks to the job interview. I explain that white socks can sabotage their chances of getting the job. They need to wear black socks.

Simon had a hard time with the black sock advice. He showed up to the workshops well-groomed. Simon paid attention to his appearance. His white socks were clean and never worn out. The black sock advice did not make sense to him. He didn't believe it!

The group had some fun, lively debates about the black sock tip. After a few days of discussions, we had to move on to new learning. Simon still had a problem with the advice. I reminded the whole group that we make choices every day. We live with the consequences.

A few weeks later, Simon got a job interview. It was a group interview done by a panel of interviewers. After the interview, the lead interviewer asked to see everyone's socks! The interviewer pointed out the black socks on one participant. They said the black socks showed someone who paid attention to detail.

This person was Simon, the non-believer from class. He decided to wear black socks that day, just in case. Simon got the job!

Wear black socks! Why? Read below.

It is interview day! You have done everything right. You have an interview for a job you want. You feel confident!

During the interview, you stretch your legs, and your pants ride up and show off your white socks. Those glowing white socks! They don't match the dark pants and dark shoes. They stand out like a mistake! How did you not notice that?

(Any socks but black might get noticed and might be judged.)

What you wear says a lot about how much you pay attention to the little things. One of the essential abilities that employers look for is attention to detail. They want a person who is careful and serious about their work. They want someone who notices the small details. For example, that employee who sees when something needs to be cleaned or dusted, shelves that need stocking or floors that need sweeping. And takes care of the situation immediately. Pay attention to the details. Don't let your socks sabotage you!

This tip caused some fun and heated talks in my workshops. Many people didn't believe socks could make a difference in their success. I don't think we should leave anything to chance. Do you?

What kind of details do you notice about other people?

_____

_____

_____

_____

_____

MINI TIP

When you hear advice that surprises you, find out more. Exercise your research and thinking skills. Start now by going online and looking up black socks and the job interview.

SKILLS AND ABILITIES

The following tips are about becoming better at what we do.

- Remember, take every opportunity to learn new things every day.
- Find training that will help you with your work goals.
- Be a lifelong learner. Never stop looking for learning opportunities.
- Learn and practice skills your skills every chance you get.

Every day is full of opportunity. Look for ways to increase your success.

TIP №13
Hands-on Skills Impress

As a child, we learned to do many things like:
- **Tie our shoes, print our name, and colour a picture.**
- **Ride a bike, rollerblade, skateboard, or ice skate.**
- **Make sandwiches and bake cookies and cakes.**
- **Play the piano, flute, or drums.**

We were not born with the ability to do these things. We had to learn how and then keep practicing.

Hands-on Skills and Work
Hands-on skills are things we learn at home, in school, at work, and in life. We gain them by being shown and trained.

Volunteer
If you want to increase your job skills, look for volunteer positions. Look for volunteer opportunities in places like the local theatre group, animal shelter, recreation center, or library. Places that help people often have volunteer programs. Think about where you live. Look in your local newspaper for places to volunteer or ask someone for ideas.

Job Training
You don't need all the job skills before an employer hires you. You can learn skills on the job. Some employers are prepared to train employees. Some employers even prefer to hire untrained staff so that they can teach them to do things their way. It is like a training program while earning a paycheck!

A job in a restaurant is a place where you will learn lots of workplace skills!

Here are some restaurant skills:
- Greeting and talking to customers.
- Taking customer orders.
- Busing the table (cleaning tables).
- Operating a cash register.
- Doing cash, debit card, and credit card transactions.
- Taking dinner reservations.
- Deep frying and grill cooking.
- Making salads, desserts, burgers, and sandwiches.
- Prepping food, cutting, and chopping.
- Mixing drinks (if the restaurant serves alcohol).
- Operating a commercial dishwasher.
- Taking inventory and ordering stock.
- Cleaning the kitchen, bathrooms, and restaurant area to health standards.

Did you know employers appreciate the training and skills people have learned in fast-food restaurants? They know that if a person has done that job, they work quickly and listen well. This is valuable to the employer. A fast-food restaurant is an excellent first job for anyone!

What other restaurant skills can you think of?

_____

_____

_____

_____

_____

Take Certificate Training

Skills are also learned by taking training classes. Find classes that you get certificates for. This training teaches you how to do something special in the workplace. You become **certified** to do a task. Look at job postings to see what type of certificates the employer wants.

Certificate training may cost money, but it pays off in the end.

1. See if there are programs in your town that help pay for the cost of training.
2. Find the money to pay for training by using the money you spend on hobbies or habits. Things like renting movies, gaming, or smoking.
3. If you are asked what you want as a gift, ask for training.

Some employers may pay for training after you are hired. Don't wait. Get training as soon as you can. Find out what employers want in their types of workplaces.

Here are some training certificates that impress employers:
• Driver's license.
• First Aid courses.
• Workplace safety courses.
• Food handling safety courses.
• Safe serving of alcohol courses.

Find out what certificates are required where you live.
Take charge of your training.

Apply to All Those Jobs

Read job postings. Look at the skills, abilities, and education the employer wants. If you are missing skills or certificates, still apply for the job. Try to figure out how you might fit.

Ask yourself these questions:
1. Do I have skills or abilities from my work at home, hobbies, or school?
2. Have I done jobs that will help me learn this one faster than someone else?
3. Is it a job that I can learn hands-on?
4. Is there a place I can get the certificates needed for the job?

Always apply for the job. Let the employer decide if you are not a good fit.

Computer Skills Are Important

Smartphones and computers are a big part of life. Lots of people are pretty good at using their technology. Most people know how to use their smartphone for social media, apps, email, and texting. These skills are valuable in the workplace. Even restaurant jobs use technology, with servers using apps and tablets for orders.

Continue to work on your computer skills. Look for computer programs that are valuable in many jobs. Companies have office tasks, and if you want to move up in the company, learn computer skills.

Never Stop Learning

Take training programs and get certificates for different types of work. Go to college or university. People who choose to learn new things are valuable to employers.

What skills do you want to learn first?

_____

_____

_____

_____

_____

MINI TIP

A great way to do a job search is to work with a friend who wants to find a job. Use this book. Work together and help each other. You will both build confidence and keep each other focused. It is like having a workout partner. Only your goal is to find a job!

TIP №14
People Skills Decide

How does it make you feel when you walk by someone, they look up, make eye contact, and you both smile? This moment of positive connection can feel good. Being friendly is a valuable people skill.

People skills come from wanting to be the best person we can be. It is how we choose to show up in life. People skills are manners, respect, and maturity. It is who we are when no one is around. It is how we act when there is nothing to gain. Be kind, caring, dependable, and put others first. It matters. Most important— people skills can't be faked!

People Skills are Behaviour Skills

Why are people skills so important? Because we want to be around others who are polite, kind, and caring. We want to work with people we can trust, are supportive, and are easy to be with. We even need good people skills to do virtual jobs. Even through the internet, people can tell if you care.

People skills cannot be taught! They can only be improved. They come from a place inside of us. People skills are how we choose to live our lives and how we treat others. They are a code of conduct that we choose because we care about ourselves and others. They are manners, respect, and maturity.

People skills are vital skills to an employer. Why? Answer these questions to see:

1. **Do you invite just anyone into your home?**
   Yes or No
   Why?_____

2. **Why do you share your time with only certain people?**
   Answer: _____

3. **Have you had people in your house who you didn't want in it?**
   Yes or No
   How did that make you feel?_____

4. **Do you have things you will and won't put up with in your home?**
   Yes or No
   What are those things?_____

5. **Is a stranger off the street welcome in your house?**
   Yes or No
   Why?_____

Now, think about when an employer hires you.

1. You are a stranger who has come right off the street.
2. They must decide if they trust you enough to invite you into their workplace. The business where they make their living.
3. They must trust that you care about their customers and look after their business.
4. They hope that you will get along with their other employees
5. They need you to be honest and trustworthy.

Examples of excellent people skills:

Is Accountable

Are you a person who admits your mistakes and makes no excuses? It's hard, and sometimes it's scary or embarrassing. You aren't perfect, and mistakes can happen. Be honest, fix your errors, and learn from them.

Will Ask Questions

Do you think it is okay that you don't know or understand something? That you need to ask questions? Do you value learning from others? Questions are one of the most powerful tools for success. Don't be afraid to ask!

Doesn't Gossip

Hopefully, you are the person who doesn't talk about others and doesn't like listening to gossip. If you are feeling a bit uncomfortable right now, don't worry. Everyone has gossiped. The good news is that it is easy to stop gossip. (Read Tip # 24)

Is Friendly

Do you like meeting friendly people? Friendly people are interested in and care about others. They make sure to include everyone. Even if you are a shy person, be nice. Decide you are going to start putting yourself out there. Start by smiling and saying hello. You will meet lots of good people.

Is a Good Listener

Did you know that listening is said to be the top people skill? (More on this in Tip #19)

A good listener is a person who encourages others to talk. They listen to understand the other person, and they do not interrupt. Good listeners know that they will learn far more by listening instead of doing the talking. They also keep the confidentiality of others and don't gossip.

Has Good Time Management

Everyone has the same amount of time each day. It is how we choose to use the time that makes a difference.

If you run your life a little behind schedule, you will miss out on so much! Being late is also hard on your reputation. People will stop trusting you. Maybe you don't think it matters if you show up a bit late for an appointment, meeting, or date. For the people waiting, it matters. To them, it feels like you don't care. They don't forget.

If you have a problem showing up on time or are always late, start working on time management. Time management is self-management. Once you relate to this, you will always be on time. Be counted on to be where you say you will be when you say so. Be someone people can trust.

Time management and the workplace means you show up to work on time every day. On-time means showing up ten minutes before you start work. You need time to put your lunch away, put on your uniform (if you have one), use the washroom, or fill your water bottle. Showing up ten minutes early means you are prepared and ready to start work on time.

Make sure you commit to being on time every day. Get an alarm clock. Use the clock and timer on your phone. Employers notice who is ready to work when it starts. Also, they will fire an employee who is late all the time. Being on time is step one of being in control of your day. Others will trust you. You will keep that job. Take charge of your time management.

Time management is also about how you use your time at work. Focus on your tasks and duties. If you run out of things to do, ask your supervisor for more work. Never stand around doing nothing. There is always something to clean or organize. Stay busy and go above and beyond what you are asked to do.

Is Reliable

Have you ever had a person let you down? Feels awful. Doesn't it? If it happens a lot, you become so tired of the apologies. A way to destroy any relationship is to make promises and not follow through.

Be reliable. It is that simple! Be the person who does what they say they will do every time. No excuses. Be honest, and don't make promises you don't intend or cannot keep.

Is a Team Player

People who play team sports or online team-based games know what team player means. Everyone must work together to win. Being a team player in the workplace is just as important. Be a person who can get along with others, is friendly, and looks for opportunities to help others. If you are like this, you are super valuable to employers. They know hiring you will have a positive impact on their workplace. Be a team player!

What people skills do you want to work on? Write them down below.

_____

_____

_____

_____

_____

_____

_____

Don't Forget

To an employer, who we are rather than what we can do matters most. Employers know they can teach us how to run a cash register, stock shelves, make a burger, or enter data in a computer. Those are hands-on skills.

Employers know that they can't teach us to be good people. That comes from inside us. Be friendly, get comfortable talking to people, and practice every chance you get!

Remember

Your people skills, or lack of them, will determine whether you get the job. Those same skills will decide if you keep the job. Choose to be the best person you can be.

MINI TIP

Pay close attention to how you show up in the world. Be kind. Care about your reputation. Make a deal with yourself to be the best you can be. Do this for you!

TIP №15
YOU Have Your Own Learning Needs

Starting a new job means there will be lots to learn. You may feel excited and anxious about your first day. You might be worried about how things will go. You might have some worries about whether you can do the job. You might wonder where your confidence went! This is how most people feel before starting a new job. Don't worry, you've got this!

One way to help make your first days easier and increase your confidence is to understand that you have your own way of learning. Decide how best you learn and then ask to be taught that way.

People learn best by:
- Watching others.
- Reading instructions.
- Writing things down (taking notes).
- Listening to others explain things.
- Trying something under supervision.

Everyone has their best ways to learn. For example, I like to be shown how to do something, given written instructions, use questions, and then try to do it with my trainer watching.

Finally, the method of learning must match what is being learned.

For example:

- It is hard to learn about what different types of dogs look like without seeing pictures of them.
- It is impossible to learn about different spices without smelling or tasting them.
- Playing tennis is the best way to learn the sport.
- A step-by-step recipe is needed to make cookies.
- To learn to speak a different language, you must hear it.

Practice all learning methods so you can use them when you need them.

When Training:

1. Look at training as a step-by-step process. Try not to look at the entire task, or you might become overwhelmed. Break it down into smaller steps.
2. Take lots of notes.
3. If permitted, use the camera on your phone to take pictures while learning.
4. Ask lots of questions.
5. Draw a picture of the steps.
6. Watch your trainer do it once or a few times.
7. Ask for practice in front of your supervisor or trainer.
8. When you get home, write down things you want to ask your trainer the next day.
9. Practice at home if that works. Set up a learning or practice place that makes you feel comfortable.
10. Look up any words you don't understand.
11. Make the information and instructions easier by rewriting them in your own words.
12. Ask your co-workers for help.
13. Stay motivated—remember why you're learning the information!

The first few weeks are the hardest. Stay in the moment and try not to worry. Ask lots of questions. Remember to say thank you to the people who help you. It won't take long before you will be comfortable and know the job.

Who has helped you learn new things?

_____

_____

_____

_____

_____

MINI TIP

Use your smile, say hello, and be kind. Employees in your new workplace often become your friends. Co-workers may walk together at lunch or meet after work. Your co-workers are the best people to get help from while learning the job right. Ask them to share what works for them. Most will be happy to help you out.

TIP №16
Skills Security,
Not Job Security

Continue to build on your skills and abilities. Even when you are working! Especially when you are working!

Jobs are never promised forever. They could end at any time for reasons we have no control over. What we do have control over are our skills and abilities.

There will be lots of opportunities that come your way. Many people don't pay attention to these opportunities when they are employed. They feel like they put in enough time and effort at work. This type of thinking can mean that if you lose your job, it will take longer to find another one. It can also lead to being stuck in the same type of job year after year.

Not learning new skills limits your chances of moving up in your workplace. When you continue to build on your skills, you may get promoted, asked to take on more responsibility and paid more.

Maybe you are not happy where you are working. Building on your skills and abilities will help you get a new job.

Learn new skills outside of your job. They don't always need to be important to your current workplace. They might be part of your bigger career plan. The skills might come from an interest you have outside of work, like a hobby.

There are lots of ways of learning new skills. You can learn in person and online. Both are valuable to your future. If you are working now, invest some of that hard-earned cash in your future!

Places to get new skills and training:
- Training might be offered in your workplace.
- Courses and certificates from your local college.
- Workshops offered in your community.
- Training that is offered at your local employment centers.
- Online workshops and webinars.
- Places you could volunteer at.
- Family member or friend who has special skills you are interested in.
- A second job in your spare time to learn something different than your current work.

Part of keeping a job and building a career is to continue to learn. You have hours left at the end of the day. A couple of them spent learning new skills will serve you well. Spend some of your spare time on your future.

What types of skills and training do you want to learn?

_____

_____

_____

_____

_____

MINI TIP

A great way to build confidence while looking for work is to become trained in something workplaces need. Get a basic first aid certificate and keep it up to date. All businesses need a staff member to have first aid.

After that, be curious and creative, and go after new training and skills. You will grow as a person; others will be impressed with you.

TIP №17
Education and Training

Never stop learning. Education helps you get and keep a job.

You could get the certificates for jobs you are interested in before handing out resumes. For example, you cannot work in jobs handling food without a food safety certificate in British Columbia. The food safety certificate means you understand how to work with food safely. This increases your chances of being hired for fast food restaurants, restaurants, delicatessens, bakeries, and any other job where food is made or served. You will have a jump on other people applying for the job who don't have the certificate.

Job Market or Labour Market Research

To find out about what types of certificates you need to work in different jobs, you can research this on the internet. This type of research, called Labour Market Research, will tell you how many jobs are available in any career and what kind of skills, abilities, and education are needed.

Prepare for College or University

If you want to go to college or university, do career research. Before you take out a student loan or pay for an expensive education, be sure you understand the career you are interested in. College and universities cost money, and they take time. You don't want to be halfway through a program and decide you have made a mistake. Worse than that, you find out that there are hardly any jobs after graduation. I have worked with people this has happened to!

Before committing to an educational program, answer the questions below. Be honest with yourself.

Write down your answers:
1. Why does this career interest me?

_____

_____

_____

2. Do I know and understand the tasks and duties in the day-to-day job?

_____

_____

_____

3. Am I choosing this because it is a passion of mine, or does someone else want this for me?

_____

_____

_____

4. Am I okay giving up time to focus on my studies?

_____

_____

_____

5. How will I afford to live while I am going to school?

_____

_____

_____

6. Do I have a support system while going to school? Who are they?

_____

_____

_____

7. Am I willing to move to where the jobs are after college or university?

_____

_____

_____

Find out how many jobs will be available after graduating. If you don't want to move away for work, find out if there are jobs where you live.

Informational Interviews
Get the questions above answered by doing informational interviews. Informational interviews are a valuable tool for job search and career research. You can interview people who work in the jobs and careers you are interested in.

Hear from the Experts

Find out who to talk to and then ask them for an informational interview. People love to talk about what they do at work. Most people are willing to give you some of their time and support. Remember, they had to look for their first job.

Prepare for an informational interview like you would for a job interview.

1. Set a date and time to meet with the person.
2. Bring along your resume, questions, and note paper.
3. If a face-to-face interview isn't possible, you can set up a phone call or use an internet program and talk over the computer.
4. If a meeting doesn't work, some people will answer your questions if you send them by email.

The person you are interviewing doesn't know what information you want. Practice the interview with someone before your actual meeting. The practice will help you better understand the questions you are asking. You want to be as prepared and confident as you can be.

Remember, whether you are meeting face-to-face or online, don't be late! These interviews are just as important as a job interview. I have worked with people who have done informational interviews that led to employment! The person they interviewed was so impressed they decided to offer them a job.

There is a list of informational interview questions in the Examples section at the back of the book. Choose the questions that work for you and add your own.

Sources for Job or Labour Market Research

There are lots of ways to get information about jobs and careers. Here are some:

- Interview employers to find out what schools they hire from.
- Interview people working in the jobs you are interested in.
- Research company websites and social media pages.
- Send a company's human resources person an email with questions about job opportunities, what they look for in an employee, and how they hire.
- Go on your local, regional, provincial, and federal labour market websites. (outside of Canada, the websites where you live.)
- College and university programs provide information about the jobs available after graduation.
- Interview graduates from college or university programs to see if they found work.

There are good career counsellors who can help you with your planning and decision-making. You can find them at colleges and universities. You can find them at employment agencies. Find a career counsellor and work with them. Going to college or university is a big step and one of those major life decisions. Get support. You don't have to go it alone.

What jobs or career interests you?

_____

_____

_____

_____

_____

MINI TIP

One of the worst reasons to choose a career is for the money. No amount of money will make you happy if you are stuck doing a job you hate. Going to work every morning in a job you hate feels like putting on lead boots and dragging yourself there. There are so many choices out there for you. Do something that you look forward to every day. You have a right to be happy in your job. Make it happen.

TIP №18
Volunteer

Volunteering means giving our time to others. Volunteering is good for us. It teaches skills. It increases wellness. We meet new friends. It says positive things about us. Volunteering also builds healthy communities.

When you volunteer, you:
- Grow roots in your community.
- Learn to be dependable and care about your community.
- Show you are grateful for what your community provides for you.
- Show you are willing to give back to your community.
- Show you are an active and motivated person with goals.

Volunteering provides you with:
- A sense of belonging.
- Personal growth.
- A place to meet new people and experience new things.
- Self-confidence and self-esteem.
- Connections to people in careers you might be interested in.
- A place to learn new skills.
- A place to try different types of work.
- Free education—volunteer agencies may pay for training.
- Opportunities to practice your people skills.
- Recent work history for your resume.
- Valuable references for employment.
- Fun.

Think about all the opportunities there might be to volunteer in your community. They are easy to find. Start by asking family and friends if they know of places to volunteer. Check your local paper and look online. See if your community has a volunteer placement program.

Ideas to Check Out:
- Youth programs.
- Seniors' centers.
- Animal rescue organizations.
- Food banks or soup kitchens.
- Homeless shelters.
- Literacy agencies.
- Cultural events.
- Local theatres.

Find out about the volunteer opportunities in your community and write them down below:

_____

_____

_____

_____

_____

Did you know that business owners volunteer? They give back because they know how important volunteering is. If you get out and volunteer, you will get to meet them and grow your network.

There is every reason to volunteer and no reason not to. Do this for you and your community.

Where would you like to volunteer?

_____

_____

_____

_____

_____

MINI TIP

Give volunteering a chance and see if you like it. It is a great place to meet new friends of all ages. It is a place to meet people who care and enjoy what they are doing in life. Set up an informational interview at a place that takes volunteers and find out what is available.

TIP №19

Listening is Communication

We might think that people who talk the most are the best communicators. They can come across as being super friendly and have something important to say about everything. However, talking a lot does not mean good communication.

Listening is an important communication skill. When we listen, we learn. Successful people know that when they pay attention, they can learn something new from anyone they talk to. They listen out of curiosity and respect. Good listeners don't feel they need to impress others by talking. Try to get to know the listeners. They have much to offer.

Someone with poor listening skills:
- Seems to never stop talking.
- Doesn't give others a chance to speak.
- Interrupts.
- Think they know what the person is going to say next. They interrupt and finish the sentence. Often, they say the wrong words.
- They are focused on speaking and stop listening to the person talking, missing what is said.

Sometimes, we may think we need to have a bright comment or opinion in a conversation to fit in. Or we may feel uncomfortable with silence and try to fill it with words. Or if we don't understand something, we pretend that we do. None of this makes us good at communicating.

When you listen, you become a good communicator.

You use good listening skills when you:
• Use eye contact.
• Don't interrupt.
• Watch the other person's facial expressions, how they are standing, and move their hands.
• Pay attention to the tone and pitch of the person talking.
• Wait before asking questions for understanding.
• Ask to move to a quiet place if you cannot hear.
• Wait to comment until you are sure the person talking has finished.

Being a good listener is part of being an excellent employee.

If you listen, you will:
• Learn faster.
• Be able to ask good questions.
• Give the best customer service.
• Make a better team member.
• Have safer work practices.
• Understand your job better.
• Have more ideas.
• Know more about the company you work for.

Listening Means Great Customer Service
As a good listener, you will be good at customer service. You will pay attention to what the customer is asking. You will be able to understand what they want. You will know what questions to ask to understand the customer's needs. Customers notice this, and they will appreciate your excellent service!

Most importantly, employers recognize good listening skills. They know that listening is part of good customer service. They will hire someone who listens well before hiring a talker.

What will you do to improve your listening skills?

_____

_____

_____

_____

_____

MINI TIP

People who walk around all day with headphones listening to music or podcasts are missing out on their lives. They miss hearing what is going on in the world around them. They can't meet people with headphones in. They are not present and in the moment. Life passes them by! If this sounds like you, put those headphones away and join the world around you.

TIP №20
Computer Skills

Computers are in every workplace, school, and job site. Computer skills are needed for banking, making appointments, registering for services, and shopping. Companies serve their customers online. You need computer skills.

Most people now have a smartphone. They know how to text, use social media, look up information online, watch videos, listen to podcasts, play games, take pictures, and make calls. These are all skills, but they are not enough for some workplaces.

Some workplaces use computers every day. Employers want their employees to be able to use online tools like calendars, email programs, and virtual meeting software. Many companies have databases to store their information. Employees must be able to learn them. They also need to be able to type documents.

Look into the computer skills needed for the jobs you are interested in.

1. Ask people you network with what computer skills they need for their jobs.
2. Ask employers what computer skills they require for their workplaces.

Find a way to get those computer skills.

Try to get a laptop as soon as you can afford one. It is hard to learn computers without one. Find some support. Find a computer class or someone to teach you. Set some time aside every day and commit to practice. You won't regret it.

Learn to type (word process). Many desk jobs require keyboarding skills. Some employers want to know how fast you can word process. There are lots of free online typing practice sites to help you out. Some of them are set up like games to make it fun. Spend time on these, building your skills.

Many employers now consider computer skills as basic job skills. Learn about computer software programs that help with business letters, money records, calendars, and online communication. I used a software program to write this book. College and university students must use computer software for their classes.

Practice computer and typing skills using the computer for personal interests.

On a computer, you can:
- Keep a journal.
- Organize your appointments.
- Track your fitness.
- Type out your job search information.
- Write letters.
- Keep recipes.
- Keep your research.
- Write poems, song lyrics, or a book.
- Use the computer to store other interests you have.

Once you start learning computer skills, you can look for new types of work. There are lots of careers that require good computer skills. Some people make their entire living working from home on their computer.

Starting now, what do you need to do to improve your computer skills?

_____

_____

_____

_____

_____

MINI TIP

It is necessary to have balance in your life. Balance screen time with some exercise. Get up and stretch. Go for a walk in the fresh air. Spend the evenings on self-care. What is one thing you will start doing for self-care right now?

TIP №21
The School of Retail

Sometimes, it is hard to figure out what to do for work. We may have to start somewhere very different than our dream job. That is okay! Every job we have will teach us valuable skills and abilities that we didn't have before. Everything we learn will help us build our careers. A job is an opportunity to learn that pays you!

The School of Retail
Working in retail is an excellent example of an opportunity to learn so many skills. Let's take a closer look.

Retail stores sell things. There are so many different types of retail stores that it is easy to find one you could relate to working in. Retail stores do the most hiring after food service jobs.

Check out the opportunities below.

Types of Retail Stores
- Clothing.
- Shoes.
- Make-up and hair products.
- Sports equipment.
- Computers and technology.
- Office supplies and furniture.
- Art and craft supplies.
- Food and drinks.
- Health products and medicine.
- Pet food and supplies.

- Snacks and lottery.
- Furniture.
- Tools and equipment.
- Paint and building supplies.
- Jewelry.
- Cars and trucks.
- Plants and garden supplies.

Types of Jobs
- Cashier.
- Customer service and product returns.
- Filling online orders.
- Ordering products.
- Pricing, displaying products, and stocking shelves.
- Bookkeeping, payroll, and banking.
- Delivering to customers.
- Unloading trucks.
- Light duty cleaning and janitorial.
- Shipping and receiving.
- Order picking.
- Inventory.
- Loss prevention/security.

People Skills
- Active listening.
- Ability to adapt.
- Attention.
- Conflict resolution.
- Creativity.
- Decision-making.
- Dependability.
- Effective communication.
- Empathy.

- Friendliness.
- Listening.
- Asking questions.
- Open-mindedness.
- Patience.
- Quick thinking.
- Understanding behaviours and feelings.
- Understanding needs.
- Time management.

Hands-on Skills
- Setting up displays.
- Stocking shelves.
- Pricing items.
- Cash register, credit card, and debit transactions.
- Product knowledge.
- Product rotation.
- Product sourcing.
- Purchasing.
- Shipping and receiving.
- Bookkeeping.
- Cash handling.
- Invoicing.
- Management.
- Marketing.
- Operations.
- Ordering.
- Payroll.

Write down the types of stores and their names that are near you:

_____

_____

_____

_____

_____

Did You Know?

People who work in retail move up into management jobs and learn business skills. Some go on to open their own store. A job in retail provides hands-on business education while you earn a paycheck!

What type of retail store would you like to work in?

_____

_____

_____

_____

_____

MINI TIP

Treat every job as a valuable education that you didn't pay for. Learn as much as you can from customers, co-workers, and management. Ask lots of questions and keep a job journal. Successful people start out somewhere very different than where they ended up.

TIP №22
Get Your Driver's License

If you have your driver's license, congratulations! It is a valuable accomplishment. It is an investment in your future. If you don't have your driver's license, consider it now.

No matter how you feel about getting a driver's license, you can take the first step. You can start studying for your learner's permit. See if you can get the book from your driver's licensing office or library. Go online and look for a website with the course. The first step requires nothing more. You can set this goal and work on it.

Once you have the study guide or the internet site, put aside time to study.

Many employers pick a job seeker with a driver's license over someone without one. Why? Because an employee with a driver's license and access to a vehicle does not have to depend on other ways to get to work. They don't need to use buses, rely on rides from family or friends, bike, or walk. In any weather, they can show up on time.

Not able to afford a car? Get a driver's license anyway. Your driver's license is still valuable to the employer. It means you can drive during work hours for them. Maybe there is a delivery to make or supplies to pick up. Sometimes, the employer will lend you their car, or they may have a company car they let you use.

Some entry-level jobs have delivery duties like:
- Pizza cooks.
- Dishwasher/bus person in a restaurant.

- A stock person in a grocery store.
- Building supply store clerk.
- Auto parts store clerk.

Lots of jobs may come with driving duties. A car cleaner and detailer must have a driver's license to move cars in and out of the car wash.

Do some research. Talk to people who drive.

Ask them:
- How long they have been driving?
- What do they like about driving?
- What opportunities has driving given them?
- How did they feel when they first started driving?
- If they have any driving advice.

Fear of Driving

If you fear driving, I still encourage you to take the first step and study for the learner's permit. Your fears are real to you. They come from somewhere, and they feel powerful. They can also control you, and that does not feel good either. Fears hold you back from achieving your goals.

A thing about fears is that they are about what you think might happen in the future. The mind takes charge and creates a story. Think about this for a few minutes.

Fear can be a story you created in your mind from worry.

Fear is a mix of what you hear, read, and have experienced.

Fear is about thinking something will happen in the future that probably won't.

What does happen is that fear controls your choices here and now. It stops you from moving forward. Fear messes up your decision-making, planning, confidence, and self-esteem.

People have shared why they don't have a driver's license.

Here are a few top reasons:
- Fear of driving and causing an accident.
- Fear of the other driver causing an accident.
- No idea how to start to get a license and had no one to help them.
- No interest in driving. They are fine walking, busing, or riding with someone else.
- No money to pay for the costs of driving.
- Driving is harmful to the environment.
- They get along fine without a license.

These are all valid reasons. But after digging a bit deeper, most people admitted that fear of driving was the main reason behind their decision not to get a driver's license.

Where to Start
If you fear driving, a driving school is excellent support. Driving schools are very good at helping new drivers become confident and capable. Practice under the watchful eyes of a teacher will help you become a good driver. Find out where the driving schools are where you live.

Cost
Driving lessons can be expensive. Don't let that be an excuse for why you can't get your license. There are ways to find the money to take lessons if you want this. First, go over your spending habits. You likely spend money on things you don't need.

Here is a short list of where you can cut back on spending:
- Fast food.
- Junk food.
- Cigarettes.
- Alcohol.
- Video games and apps.
- Movies and music apps.
- Magazines and books.
- Clothes and shoes.
- Makeup, nails, and eyelashes.
- Hobbies.

Add other extra spending to the list:
1.
2.
3.
4.
5.
6.

Do Odd Jobs

Find odd jobs like cleaning yards, mowing lawns, cleaning houses, childcare, and pet sitting. What other jobs can you think of?

Cash as Gifts

If family or friends give you gifts for birthdays, Christmas, or other special celebrations, tell them you are saving for driving lessons. Maybe they will gift you cash towards your goal.

The Expense of Driving

Driving is expensive. Interestingly, this is one of the times when people think in the moment and not in the future. They tell themselves they will never be able to afford a car or car insurance, so why bother getting a license? They forget that in the future, they could earn more money.

The Real Story

In my years of helping people find work, I have watched them get passed up for jobs they wanted and would be good at because they didn't have a driver's license.

It is a fact that having a driver's license will get you a job faster than not having one. A job means you are earning money. Money means that you might be able to afford a car and insurance. And that day might be sooner than you think!

Read about Jessie's experience in the Example section.

How do you get around in your community right now?

_____

_____

_____

_____

_____

MINI TIP

Maybe you have a car, or someone at your job does. Ridesharing is something that could help you and your co-workers. Everyone pays a small weekly fee to the driver for gas and repairs. The driver picks each person up along the route and takes them home. Remember, you must have good time management. People who are always late do not last long in a ride share.

GET SERIOUS ABOUT LIFE

The following tips are about building on our success. We need to pay attention to how we live our lives. Our choices make a difference as we become employed and start our careers.

- Always have high standards and values.
- Remember, honesty is essential for trust.
- Respect for others is necessary for building successful relationships.
- Surround yourself with people who care.

We make choices every day. Trust yourself and make choices that improve your life.

TIP № 23
Social Media

Social media is part of life for many people. It is also a very public place that is forever.

Social Media
Most people who own a smartphone or computer go on social media sites. Social media sites are fun. It is easy to spend large parts of the day scrolling them. These sites encourage people to share their personal life, thoughts, feelings, likes, and dislikes. Some people are happy to share a little too much.

Beware of how you use social media!
What you share online and the pages you follow give an impression of who you are. It might not be a good impression if you are not mindful of what you are posting.

Social Media and Employment
Many employers will look on social media to check out job applicants. It is so important to be very careful with what you post. Every post says a little about who you are. The employer will make assumptions about your personality, values, beliefs, integrity, and self-worth based on your social media.

Have a look at what people see on your site:
- Your selfies and what your face and actions say.
- Check out the background in your pictures and videos.

I watched a cooking video and was shocked because the person's kitchen was filthy. I couldn't believe they would post a video like that and not realize that people would notice their gross kitchen.

- Be careful which pages you like or share. Stay away from pages that contain content that could be racist, discriminate, or sexually offensive.
- Don't share content from other posts unless you know where it comes from and can trust it.
- Never use social media to complain about a product or service. Contact the company directly.
- Never belittle, bully, or shame others on social media. Put yourself in their shoes.
  (Review Tip # 24 on Gossip)

See If You Are Online

If you are on social media, search your name online. You might be surprised by what comes up!

The Fake World

Only paid influencers benefit from sharing about themselves. They are careful about what and how they share content. They are running an online business. They are looking for followers to buy things. They aren't looking for friends or employment.

Don't Forget

You have control over your social media.

Many successful people have moved off social media. You have that choice. Limit the time you spend on social media and control your content. You will be safer and happier doing both.

Are there things on your social media sites you want to clean up?

_____

_____

_____

_____

_____

MINI TIP

A common excuse I hear people say is, "But I have no time."

Everyone has the same amount of time every day. Think about how much time you spend on your phone, computer, TV, or video game console. The less time you spend online, the more time you have for your goals. Life is about doing things, not watching others do life. How you choose to use time will decide what you get done.

TIP №24
Gossip Hurts YOU AND Others

Oh yes. There must be a tip on gossip. Everyone gossips from time to time. Some more than others.

Everyone listens to gossip. Everyone likes the "news" about actors, singers, and other famous people. Much of what you learn about them, however, is gossip. You will never know the truth because you can't go to them and ask.

It would be impossible to tell people to quit gossiping altogether. It is human nature. It is how people learn information. Some types of gossip can be helpful.

Gossip
A snoopy neighbour makes it their job to keep track of what goes on in the neighbourhood. They are always gossiping about all the neighbours. You don't pay much attention to them. It is frustrating, but you can avoid them. Maybe one day, they might prevent a robbery or save a life because they are so interested in what their neighbours are doing.

Maybe through gossip, you have heard that a restaurant has been serving unsafe food and people are getting sick. That type of gossip might be helpful. You can decide how to handle the information and make your own choices.

Toxic Gossip

Gossip that hurts others is wrong. It is one of the most toxic and self-defeating behaviours you can participate in. It is mean and cruel, and it has no value. Gossip doesn't help resolve problems. It creates more.

Fact

People who gossip are often angry, lonely, jealous, hurt, and sad. They are people who try to make themselves feel better by spreading nasty rumours about others. Gossip will always get back to the person who is being gossiped about. In extreme instances, criminal charges might happen.

Live Your Life

People that don't gossip are happy with themselves. They focus on their own lives. They are too busy to bother about what others are doing or saying. They don't care to get involved in spreading gossip.

A Boundary Tool

Here are two questions to help you set boundaries with someone who comes to you with toxic gossip.

Stop the person as soon as they start to gossip and ask:
1. "Please tell me why you are telling me this?"
2. "What does this have to do with me?"

These two questions ask the person to explain why they are telling you the information. They must look at what they are saying. Hopefully, they realize that it is none of your business or theirs. Politely tell them that you are not interested, then change the topic.

Part of being a good role model is how you treat others. Refusing to gossip is leadership behaviour. There is never a time when we have an excuse to spread cruel gossip.

Remember this **life lesson**. It is never too late to be your best self.

How will you set boundaries around gossip?

_____

_____

_____

_____

_____

MINI TIP

Start a gratitude journal. Being grateful for the small things in life brings happiness. Write about them every day. What is the first thing you will put in your gratitude journal?

TIP Nº25
Your References

References are one of our most important assets. Employers will check our references as the final step before offering us a job.

An employer can ask you for a reference for any jobs on your resume. They typically pick your latest jobs. Employers know that some people may not be honest on their resume about the dates they worked or what their job was. That is why they ask for some proof of employment. Have a list of references and their contact number ready on a separate paper.

There are two types of references. Personal references from community members who know you. Work references from past employers that confirm your work history and work performance.

It is a good idea to have more than one reference. It is your responsibility to keep your reference list up to date by having the correct contact information. It is up to you to stay in touch with your references. When you can, keep them in your network.

Make sure you ask before using someone as a reference. If a prior employer does not give references, they can confirm that you worked during the time you said on the resume. Try to have other references.

Gather Your References
1. Your work history and volunteer places for a work reference. Write the names down.
2. Include your volunteering at school.
3. Most teachers and instructors will give references.

4. Decide who you think will be willing to give you a reference.
5. Speak to that person directly.
6. Ask them for a reference that includes your work ethic, skills, and abilities.
7. You might want to describe the work you did for them to help them remember.
8. Ask your references if they would write you a reference letter for your portfolio.

Put the names of people you think of below:

_____

_____

_____

_____

_____

Past employers want to know you are using them. Remember to ask them each time. Tell them who will be contacting them. Tell them what job you are applying for. If your reference is prepared, they can give a much better picture of you.

If you have no work-related references, it's okay. You can use personal references. Personal references are often called character references. It is up to you to ask people to be a character reference. If you know businesspeople in the community, ask them.

Teachers or well-known community members might be a character reference. Choose people who can talk about who you are as a person. They will describe your people skills that are valuable to an employer.

Try not to use family references unless they are all you have. People think that family will say good things because they are related. If you must use family, explain why you chose them. Maybe you did odd jobs for them, or they are business owners or leaders in the community.

Example of a Character Reference

As a job search trainer, I have been a character reference for many participants in my employment programs. For some, I was the most recent reference they had. I could not tell employers about them as an employee. However, I was able to talk about their participation in the workshops and my program.

As a character reference, I could talk about things I observed, including:

- They talked out in the group and shared ideas.
- Came to class prepared.
- Worked well in a team.
- Participated in the activities.
- Paid attention to grooming and hygiene.
- Showed up on time.
- Had good attendance.
- Cleaned up at the end of the day.

If I agreed to give a reference, it would be because I would not hesitate to recommend that person for the job.

You must respect your references! They are often busy people.

1. Contact the person and ask if they will be a reference. They will tell you yes or no.
2. After that, contact this person each time you use them as a reference. Find out if they are still willing to be a reference.
3. Prepare the person by sending them your resume, cover letter, and the job posting you are interviewing for. This

gives them time to think about what they will say about you that is relevant to the job.

Important Note

References are private and confidential and should remain so unless you need to use them. It has been a practice to advise job seekers to hand in their references with their resumes. I do not recommend this. Keep references on a separate sheet of paper. If you are asked for your references when putting in a resume, that is when you must give them. If this happens, you need to let your references know right away.

Some reasons we should not hand out our references unless asked:

1. The employer can check your references even before calling you for an interview or considering you for the job. This is not an ethical practice.
2. If you have handed out several resumes, your references may be contacted repeatedly as a screening process before the interview. This may become a nuisance to them.
3. If there is a disagreement with one of your references (it has happened to job seekers I worked with), and your resume is out there with your reference attached, that reference has a chance to sabotage your job search. You may never find out.
4. Your reference information is shared with people who don't need it.

Make a list of people you might ask to be a reference. Let them know you are looking for work. Most people are happy to help someone who is looking for a job.

Who will you ask first for a reference?

_____

_____

_____

MINI TIP

Things change. One of those changes is when you leave your job to move on to something new. When you do, remember to ask for a reference letter. Don't be shy. Your employer knows the value of reference letters. Most will be happy to write one for you.

TIP №26
Mentorship

Mentor: an experienced and trusted advisor.
Mentors have the skills, abilities, knowledge, and experience
to be experts in their chosen careers. Mentors are well-known
and respected by their peers. Mentors are passionate about
their work and want to give back to others.

Mentors are people who have worked in careers and have a successful work history. Mentors will share what they know about how to achieve goals. They have been there. You get the benefit of their hard work. Find yourself a mentor.

What It Feels Like to Be Mentored

Mentors will offer professional advice on your job search and career goals. A mentor will give you honest feedback on your skills and abilities. They will evaluate your strengths and weaknesses and assist you in overcoming barriers and challenges.

Mentors give positive feedback and praise where they see your strengths. When your mentor says you have what it takes, you can believe them. They are actively evaluating your skills and abilities against their years of knowledge and experience.

Connections

Mentors have valuable connections that they have made during their careers. These connections may be able to help you move forward with your goals.

What You Must Do for Your Mentor

Accountability is vital to a mentor. They will not let you waste their time, and they will not waste yours. They will expect you to give 100% to your goals and follow through on their instructions and advice. It is crucial to respect the time your mentor gives you. Do the steps and work they give you to do.

Make sure you are showing your mentor you are grateful for their support. Ask them what you can do to give back to them. This is a professional relationship and is not to be taken for granted. Having a mentor is valuable for success.

Write a list of people you think would be a good mentor for you.

_____

_____

_____

_____

MINI TIP

When you get your job, find a mentor to help you while you learn your responsibilities. Ask someone you connect with if they will be your mentor. No one has ever succeeded all alone. Remember that and ask for support. When will you ask someone to be your mentor?

JOB SEARCH

The following tips are about getting prepared for the actual job search.

- Get organized.
- Use a calendar. Keep track of your activities every day.
- Don't leave anything to chance. Be prepared for anything that comes your way.
- Don't stop until you have a job.

Every day, there are tasks to complete. It is a full-time job finding employment.

TIP № 27
Your RESUME Sparks Interest

This tip is not about how to write a resume. There are books, websites, and online courses on resume writing. There are free templates and sample resumes online. Find an employment agency that provides resume writing services and will help you. If you want to learn how to write your own, take a good resume writing course. You cannot learn to write a resume in a 1-day workshop.

Handing out your resume is the first step to getting invited for a job interview. This section tells you what should be on your resume.

The resume is an important document. Take charge of what is written on yours. It is your history. Learn what belongs on a resume and what does not.

A good resume is essential because it is the first opportunity to market your skills and impress your future employer. Your resume must be well-written and have truthful information. Refuse to let anyone convince you to put skills, abilities, or experiences that you do not have. Don't worry about your lack of experience. Everyone has a first resume. Even if they have never worked. More on that later!

What a Resume Is

A resume is a summary of your skills, abilities, and achievements. It contains your education, work history, and volunteer experience. Make sure your resume has been typed out right (formatted). There are samples on the internet of how one should look.

Speaks About You

The resume gets you an invitation to a job interview. On the resume, tell the employer which job you are applying for. Target the resume to the type of job you want. After the employer reads your resume, they will decide if they will interview you to learn more.

Remember, a resume does not get you a job. It gets you an interview!

Contains the Truth

It is necessary that you feel confident about everything that is on your resume. Be sure the person who helps you write it doesn't stretch the truth. In the job interview, you will be expected to talk in detail about when, where, what, and how you have used the skills and experience you stated on your resume.

I have read many resumes where well-meaning resume writers have said a person has skills, abilities, or experience that are false. In the interview, the employer asked the job seeker to explain a skill or task they have never done. They could not answer the question. A bad situation to be in!

Even worse, can you imagine getting a job because of false information? You show up at work without the ability to do the job. Not a good start. Always be honest about your experience.

Big Words or Jargon

Big words and jargon do not belong on resumes. When someone writes your resume and wants to put in words you are not familiar with, it is up to you to stop them. You will end up in another awkward situation in the interview. When job-related words need to be used, make sure you learn them. Use plain language as much as possible.

Keep A Copy

Once you have your first resume, save a copy on a USB flash drive. (A USB flash drive is a data storage device). Buy one. They are worth the money. You will have your base resume to add to as your career goes forward.

No computer to edit your resume? You will still have the resume on a USB flash drive to use on a public computer. If someone else is helping you with your resume, you can take the USB flash drive to them, and they can download it, or you can email them a copy from any computer.

When you get skills and training certificates, you can save them on the USB flash drive. It keeps all your important papers together, and they can be printed or emailed along with your resume if an employer asks for them.

Update Your Resume

Update your resume with new training, education, and work experience. Employers are impressed with people who continue to update their skills and are interested in learning new things.

Check for Mistakes

Always make sure someone reviews your resume. A resume with words spelled wrong or bad formatting is often passed over. Ask someone to review your resume for you, even if it has been done by a professional. Anyone can make mistakes. Avoid mistakes that can ruin your chance of getting the job.

If You Quit a Job

If you quit a job, you can put it on your resume. If you were good at the work and spent a long time there, you might want the job on your resume. Stay away from the details about the issues. Focus on the skills you learned working there.

Dismissed from a Job

Being dismissed or fired from a job is not an easy topic. It does happen. If this has happened to you, you must decide whether to put that job on your resume or leave it off. If you put the job on your resume and the employer asks for a reference for that job. You will have to give them one. You will have to explain what happened.

Sometimes, people decide to put a job they were fired from on the resume because it has valuable skills and is a big part of their work history. If this is the case, a prepared reason for the dismissal will help.

Ask Yourself These Questions:

1. What do I think my past employer will say about me if they are called for a reference?

   Answer:

   _____

   _____

   _____

   _____

   _____

2. Am I willing to go and talk to that employer about a reference? What will I say to them?

   Answer:

   _____

   _____

   _____

   _____

3. What do I remember about why I was fired?
   Answer:

   _____

   _____

   _____

   _____

   _____

4. **If asked**, what will I say about being fired?
   Answer:

   _____

   _____

   _____

   _____

   _____

Remember

You must be the one to decide if you want to include the job you were fired from on your resume. If you leave the job on the resume, be prepared to explain the valuable lesson you learned from the experience. If you learned from your mistake, the situation wasn't all bad.

Employer Contacting You

This is important! Be sure your phone number and email are correct. If the employer cannot contact you, you will miss the opportunity. This has happened!

See a sample of a basic resume in the Example section.

Key Points to Remember:

1. Don't let anyone bully you into believing you must write your resume. Find some help!
2. Know your resume and be able to talk about it.
3. Buy a USB flash drive to save copies of your resume.
4. Make sure your contact information is correct.
5. State the job you are targeting.
6. Always be completely honest on your resume.

What needs to be done so you have a good resume?

_____

_____

_____

_____

_____

MINI TIP

Just like paying attention to personal grooming, make sure the paper copies of your resume are clean, not folded, and free from stains. A crumpled or smudged resume will often be rejected because it looks like the person doesn't care about important things. Use a folder to keep your resume from getting damaged.

TIP №28
The Cover Letter is Your "Voice"

Some employers like to have resumes dropped off at their business. Some employers use email to collect resumes. We might prefer to email or resume because we don't have to talk to anyone. Emailing is less stressful than going into a business to drop off our resume. That might be true. But is this a good thing? Not really.

Sending in a resume by email means we lose the chance to show our winning personality. Remember those people skills that the employer cares about the most? They don't come across very well in an email.

That is where the cover letter comes in. When a cover letter is included with a resume, it gives you a chance to "speak" about your skills. A cover letter goes with a resume and is the first friendly, personal communication between you and the employer. The cover letter explains your interest in the job and what you bring to the position.

Cover letters can be tricky to write, so get help with them. If your cover letter is well written, you will stand out to the employer. They will learn more about you that is not on your resume. Be careful. If your cover letter is unclear or "rambles on," then the employer might not take the time to look at your resume.

The best way to describe the cover letter is that it is a tool that "talks" to the employer when you can't. It is your chance to tell them briefly how your skills and abilities match their job needs. You can give examples of what you bring to the workplace.

The job posting is your guide to writing the cover letter. The job posting describes what the employer is looking for. You can pick a couple of keywords the employer put in the job posting about what they are looking for and use them in the cover letter. Use the ones that match your skills, abilities, and experiences, and write about them. Give some details about what you can bring to the workplace.

Be clear and direct. A mistake often made is that people rewrite what is on their resume! The employer has your resume in front of them and can read it. Show the employer how your skills and abilities match the job. Don't add a bunch of words or useless information.

Think of the cover letter as your opportunity to "talk" to the people who are doing the hiring. This is when you tell them who you are and what you bring to the position.

Cover Letter Information
1. Write a sentence about who you are and why you want to work for the company.
    Answer:

    _____

    _____

    _____

    _____

    _____

2. Write a sentence about why you would be a good employee.
   Answer:

   _____

   _____

   _____

   _____

   _____

3. Write two or three sentences on how your skills, abilities, and experiences match the job tasks.
   Answer:

   _____

   _____

   _____

   _____

   _____

   _____

4. Give one or two examples of what you have done in the past that helps explain the above sentence (#3).
   Answer:

   _____

   _____

   _____

   _____

   _____

Check for Mistakes

Ask at least two people to read your cover letter for mistakes. English writing rules like grammar, punctuation, and spelling count! A poorly written cover letter will not get you a job interview.

Other Uses for a Cover Letter

A cover letter can be used to explain something on your resume that needs explaining. If you haven't worked before, have long breaks between jobs, or are making a career change, you can write about that. If you explain things about your resume, the employer doesn't have to make guesses.

Follow Instructions

When the job posting asks for a cover letter, you must include a cover letter. If the job posting says no cover letter, don't send one. Employers are looking at whether you can follow instructions.

If the job posting doesn't say either way, it is your choice. A well-written cover letter takes time. Maybe you want to get your resume in quickly because the job posting has a deadline. Then skip the cover letter and get the resume in! A good resume will work by itself. If you have the time, the cover letter is still a good idea!

There is information on cover letters in the Example section.

Practice Writing a Cover Letter

Practice helps build skills. By doing a practice cover letter, you will learn how to describe your skills and abilities and how you fit the job. Your rough draft will be valuable to the person helping you write the cover letter.

Write a Rough Copy

1. Find a job posting that you want to apply for.
2. Use the cover letter instructions in the Example section and practice writing a cover letter.

People like it when you try. They are more willing to help you with the final cover letter when you do. Ask someone you trust to read your cover letter and help you improve it.

What skills and abilities will you share with the employer?

_____

_____

_____

_____

_____

MINI TIP

Use some time to practice talking out loud about what you have done at school and work that you are proud of. Describe the steps you did. Better still, record what you say! This will help you to talk about your skills in a job interview.

TIP №29
Networking is Very Important for Success

People network. They share information with others all the time. It is sometimes done casually, like talking to friends and family about the best bike shop, gaming site, pizza place, or restaurant in town. Businesspeople network. They continue to build their contacts. This helps their business success.

Networking is Important
Networking for a job is one of the most important tools we have. Networking gets us contacts and leads that help with our job search. It lets as many people as possible know we are looking for work.

The Hidden Job Market
Job search networking means meeting new people. These contacts may have information about a business that might be hiring soon. This is called the "hidden job market." The first to know about a new job.

The hidden job market is jobs that have not been advertised. Many employers will ask their network if they know anyone looking for work. They will do this before they post the job. A business owner's network is other business owners, friends, and family. When you network, you might hear about a job before anyone else. The first to apply for the job is always a good thing!

An Example of an Employer Using Networking

Rachel, the owner of a popular restaurant called "The Bistro," is ready to hire two more servers. The restaurant is busy, and Rachel needs these new employees right away. She is willing to hire someone who has never worked in a restaurant. She likes to train her staff a certain way. Rachel would like to find her new employees without posting the job online. She doesn't have the time to go through a bunch of resumes. Rachel decides to use her network.

(Note: not a real place or employer.)

One Day of Rachel's Networking in Action

1. On the way to work, Rachel stops at a grocery store she shops in for the restaurant. She talks to her **friend who manages the store** and tells them she is looking for servers.
2. She goes to the **liquor store** and talks to the **store manager** as she picks up the alcohol for the restaurant.
3. After that, she goes and gets her hair done and **tells her stylist** she is looking for employees.
4. Then she stops at a clothing store for a new dress and tells the **salesperson and store owner** she is hiring.
5. Then she stops for gas and tells the **pump attendant** she is looking for servers.
6. She meets her friend for lunch. The **friend owns a daycare center** in town. She tells her she is ready to hire new employees.
7. Rachel tells the **server** that she is hiring at her restaurant.
8. After lunch, Rachel has a dentist appointment. She tells the **receptionist, dental assistant,** and **dentist** she is hiring new employees.
9. The next stop is Rachel's gym, where she talks to the **owner** and **trainer** about her hiring needs.

10. Rachel stops to see her mom and dad for a brief visit and shares that she is ready to hire two new servers. Rachel's **mom works in the large department** store in town. Her **dad owns the local tire store**. They both have a vast network.
11. Rachel has an early dinner with her family. Her **daughter** and **son** go to the **local high school** and **work in different retail stores** in town. Rachel's **husband** works for the local **government as a city planner**. They are all connected to many people.
12. After dinner, Rachel is off to the restaurant for the evening. She tells **her staff** that she is looking for two new servers. She asks them if they can recommend anyone they know.

Every person Rachel talked to in the one day knows she is looking for two new employees. These people will be telling their network! That is why networking is valuable.

Rachel's information will be shared by every person she met today with their network. See how the news can spread! Rachel will probably never have to write a job posting. She will get resumes coming in from her network.

If you knew someone who was part of Rachel's network, you would find out about the job because you have told everyone in your network that you are looking for work. Just like magic! That is how networking works!

How To Build a Network

It is super easy to build a network. You already have one! It is people you see and talk to in your life. It is your family, friends, and people you see during your day.

To build your network, talk with as many people as possible. Tell everyone you meet that you are looking for a job. Your network has a network! The number of people who know you are looking for work will explode!

You can share that you are looking for work on social media sites you are on. It is wise to use the privacy settings or send a private message so only the contacts you trust know you are looking for work. Keep an eye on your social media to be sure you are not being messed with.

Networking is also a great way to meet new people. It is valuable to grow your network with new people. You can do this by looking for things to do in your community. Go to public events such as art shows, local markets, fairs, and public meetings. If you feel shy, ask a friend to come with you.

Volunteering is another excellent way to build your network. When you volunteer in your community, you meet new people. Your network will expand and grow.

Get Ready to Network
The first thing to do is write down everyone you know. Your network.

Don't forget to include:
- Family.
- Friends.
- Neighbours.
- Teachers.
- Dentists.
- Doctors.
- Bus drivers.
- Store cashiers.

My Network

_____

_____

_____

_____

Steps To Follow:
1. Practice your 30-second Pitch so you can introduce yourself. **(See TIP #30 on the 30-Second Pitch)**
2. Keep notes in your job search journal about job lead information.
3. Write down any advice you get.
4. Follow up on every lead. **"Jessica said you were hiring." (Don't forget to thank Jessica later!)**
5. When you meet someone, ask if you can keep in touch.
6. Make sure to thank everyone.
7. Share your network with others.
8. Stay focused and network daily. It is up to you to help people remember you.
9. Keep a positive attitude and ask for a job.

Networking Works!
The more people that know you are looking for work, the better.

Where will you network first?

_____

_____

_____

_____

MINI TIP

Find different ways to meet people. You don't have to do this alone. Invite your friends or family to go with you to things happening in your community. Get used to being out in public. Keep smiling and talking to others. What event will you attend first?

TIP №30
How to Introduce Yourself—
The 30-second Pitch

An essential part of the job search is introducing ourselves to people. Learn to start conversations that could get you valuable job leads or even job offers!

Introducing ourselves to new people isn't easy. It takes practice, confidence, and being okay with stumbling along at first. It is helpful to write down and practice what we want to say.

In a job search, this is called a '30-second Pitch.' It is a 30-second introduction with information about us that an employer might want to know.

30-second Pitch
- Helps you to talk to a manager when you drop off your resume.
- Makes it less stressful to introduce yourself in any networking situation.
- Keeps the focus on skills, abilities, and goals.
- Helps spark interest and curiosity about you.

30-second Pitch Sample
"Hi. My name is Jordan Smith. I have just graduated. I am looking for entry-level work. I am interested in carpentry, landscaping, or restaurant jobs.

Last summer, I did trail building and clam digging. I do yard cleanup and garden work.

I am very interested in cooking. I cook most of the meals at home. A job in a restaurant kitchen would be great.

I believe in helping others and giving back to my community. I volunteer for a program that mows lawns for elders.

Would you have any suggestions for my job search?"

* * *

Use the guide below to help you write a brief introduction. You can change sentences and write what feels right to you.

Your 30-second Pitch (fill in the blanks)

"Hi. My name is _____. I am looking for employment. I am _____. I have an interest in _____. Another interest is _____. I believe in _____. I am looking for opportunities in entry-level in _____. Would you have any suggestions for my job search?"

Get Some Feedback

Ask for support and feedback from someone you trust. Time yourself and practice it in front of family or friends.

Keep your introduction to 30 seconds. Longer, and you might go off track. You want the listener to become interested in you and start asking you questions! Your confident introduction, describing who you are and what you like to do, may get you a job interview.

Who will you practice your 30-second Pitch on?

_____

_____

_____

_____

_____

MINI TIP

Car coaching is a great way to start handing out resumes. Ask a friend or family member to be your car coach. Ask them to drive you around while you hand out your resume. Have them park where they can't be seen by the employer. After you drop off your resume, you tell them how each drop-off went. Review what you did, how you greeted people, and what was said. Get them to give you some feedback. It is always easier to do something when you are not alone.

TIP №31
How to Read a Job Posting

Looking for a job is a lot of work! Be open to applying for as many different jobs rather than trying to find the perfect one. We will never really know if we like or don't like a job until we give it a chance. The best way to approach a job search is to stay focused and be open to new things.

You can apply for many different types of jobs. The job posting guides you. Break down a job posting into smaller parts to see where and how your skills and abilities fit.

How To Break Down a Job Posting
Read the job posting for **Get Fit Gym** on the next page. (Get Fit Gym is not a real place.)

Get Fit Gym – We are Hiring!

Get Fit is hiring a part-time **customer service ambassador** in our gym in Somewhere, BC.

As a **Get Fit Ambassador,** you will:
- Be an enthusiastic employee and support gym members while they enjoy their fitness workouts.
- Remind each member how important they are.
- Keep members informed of upcoming programs and events.
- Model the importance of health and fitness.

As a **Get Fit Ambassador,** you maintain a high level of professionalism and play a critical role in taking the opportunity to interact and involve all members in our fitness culture.

Responsibilities:
- Entrance Security- screen and admit members who enjoy 24-hour access to the facility.
- Inform the membership of upcoming events and contests.
- Ensure machines are wiped down after each use.
- Refill bottles of cleaner and replace cleaning towels.
- Keep restrooms clean and toilet paper and towel supplies stocked.
- Follow workplace health and safety practices and procedures.
- Do routine equipment checks during shifts to ensure safety.
- Report all maintenance issues to the Facility Manager.
- Represent Get Fit Gym as one of their ambassadors in the community.
- Assists with supply inventory and other duties as assigned.

You will have:

- Knowledge of workplace safety and janitorial training are assets.
- Excellent organization skills; team player.
- Ability to establish rapport and excellent communication with members, staff, and suppliers.
- Commitment to working in a socially inclusive environment.
- Respond with sensitivity and personal awareness to the diverse needs of all members, including visible and non-visible dimensions of diversity.
- Flexibility regarding the work schedule: shifts will include days, evenings, and weekends.

Please submit your resume and cover letter to Jim Owner at jim.owner@notreal.com
If you have any questions, contact me at 250-000-0000
Thank you for applying. Only those chosen for an interview will be contacted.

This is an entry-level job. It could be learned by anyone interested in it.

The gym job posting is full of detail. This type of posting might make you feel overwhelmed. The word **Ambassador** might scare you off. Maybe you have never been to a gym or done any customer service. Don't pass up this opportunity yet. Think about what the employer is looking for. Then, match your skills to those tasks and duties.

Break the Job Posting Down

Tasks and Duties:

- Greet members and make them feel welcome.
- Check memberships.
- Let members know what events are coming up.
- Clean machines, general cleaning, and stock supplies.
- Check that the equipment is working and report any issues.
- Count the supplies and place orders.

Pay attention to the people skills listed in the posting. They are the skills that are most important to the employer. Remember, these are the people skills that cannot be taught.

People Skills:

- Team player.
- Friendly and able to talk to customers, co-workers, and suppliers.
- Have a professional image when in the community.
- Treat everyone with respect.
- Be organized.
- Commitment to working in a socially inclusive environment.

- Respond with sensitivity and personal awareness to the diverse needs of members, including visible and non-visible dimensions of diversity.

The last 2 bullets are critical. This means this company protects the rights of every customer and employee. They care about people.

After breaking down this job posting, it is less overwhelming. You can see that this job could be learned after you are hired. Remember, employers expect to train new employees.

Don't count yourself out of jobs because you think you are not skilled or experienced enough. Let the employer decide that.

What are three different types of jobs you will apply for?

_____

_____

_____

_____

_____

MINI TIP

People like to use big words to impress others. Look up every word you don't know. When I guess the meaning of words, I am often wrong. A dictionary or the internet is the best resource for learning words on the job posting. This will help you understand what the employer wants and increase your confidence to apply for the job.

TIP №32
The Value of Every Employee

When you drop your resume off in person, you will meet employees working in the business. Remember to smile and say hi. One of those employees might play a part in you getting the job.

Business owners and managers rely on their employees for feedback about people who drop off their resumes in person.

They will ask their employee questions like:
- Did they smile?
- Did they make eye contact?
- Did they introduce themselves?
- Were they polite?
- What were they wearing?
- What did they say?

When dropping off resumes in person, dress for success, remember to smile and introduce yourself. This is the first contact you will have with the employer. Remember, you never get a second chance to make a first impression!

Jobs With a Reception Area
The reception or front desk person is often the first person you will have contact with on the phone or in person. They are the gatekeepers of the company. Their job is to look after customers, clients, and co-workers. They make sure the business runs well.

Greet the receptionist with a smile and friendly hello. Relax, smile, and speak confidently and clearly. Ask them how their day is going. That is all it takes to get the conversation going. And yes, this is when you can talk about the weather!

Be clear with the person who greets you about why you are there. Tell them that you would like to drop off a resume. Introduce yourself. Ask if the person who does the hiring is available. That would be the best person to hand the resume to.

Retail Store and Restaurant Jobs
Greet the first employee you meet with a smile and hello. Tell them you would like to drop off your resume. Ask them if you can speak to the person who does the hiring. If other employees are nearby, smile and say hello to them. After you leave, they will get together and talk about you. Give them positive things to say.

Smile and be friendly, even if you feel self-conscious or anxious. Be your best self. Everyone faces awkward moments. It can help to practice at home. Ask a friend for support.

Emailing Your Resume
If you are emailing your resume, write a short note. Greet the person by name (use Mr. or Ms. and their last name). Introduce yourself. Explain to them why you are emailing. Be sure to thank the person for taking the time to read your resume. Put your name at the bottom of the note and include your phone number below your name. Check your spelling. Ask someone to read over the email before you send it. Attach your resume and press send.

First impressions count in emails, also!

Phone Calls

The same rule applies if you are phoning. If you are making a call, be sure you have prepared what you will say. Write down what you want to say. Do not wing it.

Did you know you can hear a smile? It is true! Make sure you smile while talking.

Thank the person for their time and help. If they ask you to call back, make sure you get a date and time and call back then. Remember, you are making a first impression over the phone.

What will you say when you drop off your resume?

_____

_____

_____

_____

MINI TIP

We all have an inner voice that chatters nonstop (our thoughts). We talk to ourselves out loud. Pay attention to each negative thought or word you say. When you catch yourself saying something negative, say two positive things out loud. This exercise will give you the power to learn to focus on what is good and positive instead of going to an unhelpful place. Try it. Make sure you say it out loud so that you hear yourself. Hearing your voice helps the positive messages sink in!

TIP №33
Job Search Journal

It is a full-time job looking for work. That means it takes about five to seven hours a day to do a successful job search. All this hard work needs organization somewhere. That is where a job search journal comes in.

Part of the time, you will be working on a job search journal. The job search journal keeps all the details about your daily job search activities in one place. There will be important things to remember. Don't rely on your memory.

At the end of each day, you use your job search journal to record your:
- Type of job search (in person, networking, over the internet, job fair).
- List the jobs you applied for.
- People you talked to.
- Information from conversations.
- When you need to follow up.
- Results of calls, emails, or in-person meetings.
- Company research.
- Training research.

Use the journal so you have names, times, and dates for follow-up.
The best type of job search journal is a three-hole binder with lined paper. Print job postings and keep them. If you don't have

a binder, a notebook will do. Use a stapler or tape to keep loose pages in the right place.

In the journal:
1. Put in a monthly calendar—you can find printable calendars online for free.
2. Make a daily to-do list: where you will go, whom you will contact, and what follow-up to do.
3. Put in a copy of the job postings you are applying for with the time and date on them.
4. Write down information from your company research: site visits, internet information, and contact names.
5. Put in updated resumes and cover letters so that you remember what you sent to each employer. On the back of each, jot down notes on how you submitted them: online at the company website, in person, or by email.
6. Record details of each contact with employers—date, time, place, time spent talking, topics, results, and follow-up dates.
7. Write out the results of informational interviews. Put down what was said and any new information you learn.
8. Record your practice times and what you practiced: thirty-second pitch and interview questions.
9. List networking contacts and details of conversations.
10. Collect business cards, tape them in, and write a description beside them.
11. Record the thank you cards or notes and who and when you sent them.

Using a job search journal teaches you to be organized, pay attention to detail, and keep good records. Employers value staff who are organized and keep track of important information.

What are the first things you will write or put in your job search journal?

_____

_____

_____

_____

_____

MINI TIP

Unemployed people often become cut off from others. It is lonely being unemployed. Without a job and money, people cannot afford to do things that working people can. They may struggle with low self-esteem and self-worth, and they may even experience depressive symptoms.

When you are unemployed, treat your job search like a job. Get up at the same time every morning. Have breakfast before starting your job search tasks. Take a break for lunch, then continue until the end of the workday. Spend at least five hours a day.

If you are serious about finding a job, use this tip book. Fill the five hours a day on job search tasks. Go to bed early. Get up and repeat. You will learn and grow during this time. And you will find a job!

TIP №34
Career Portfolio

Start a career portfolio right now. The portfolio is a valuable job search tool because it contains samples of your accomplishments. Those samples are your achievements. They are certificates, letters, samples of work and pictures.

Career portfolios include your skills, abilities, education, and achievements. Include examples from special clubs, sports, school, training, volunteerism, and employment.

Use a black or white three-ring binder. Buy some three-ring plastic page protectors. Keep your binder safe and in good condition. It holds proof of your hard work and achievements.

Here is a sample list of things you might find in a career portfolio:
- Newspaper clippings.
- Certificates of participation (clubs, events, groups, programs, etc.).
- An updated resume.
- School records.
- School awards.
- Samples of your writing.
- Samples of your projects.
- Photographs of your work.
- Newspaper articles with you in them.
- A sample cover letter you have written.
- Letters of recommendation talking about your achievements (include employers, neighbours, friends, and teachers).

- Your participation in community activities (courses, cultural clubs/organizations, fund-raising events, and other activities specific to your community).
- A written summary of your experiences.
- Photos of your experiences.
- Include any other information about your participation in the community.

I have a letter of reference from my first job when I was sixteen! I still have my letter in my portfolio. It may not be relevant to my career today, but the words in this letter still mean a lot. The words talk about who I was as a young person in the workplace.

If you have a job search portfolio, bring it to the job interview. If you get an opportunity, you can show proof of your work as you talk about it.

What do you already have for your portfolio?

_____

_____

_____

_____

_____

MINI TIP

If you are good with computers, you might want to learn how to do a digital portfolio. You can share access to your digital portfolio with anyone you choose. With all the different online careers, a digital portfolio is a good option for showing your achievements.

TIP №35
Calling Cards

Calling cards are a valuable networking tool. You are in the business of finding a job. You could use a business card for your job search. You can give people your card. Then they have a way to contact you.

Businesspeople use a business card. It has the company's name, the person's name, phone number, email address, and website. There is some information about the business. They leave them with people they meet.

Calling Cards

You may not always have a resume with you. There will be times when you are out in the community that you wish you had. If you had a calling card, you could give it to the contact you met.

A calling card is the same size as a business card and fits nicely in a pocket or purse. It contains your name and contact information. In the place of the business name, you include information like your skills and abilities.

If you have computer skills, you can find sites online that you can use to create your calling cards. If you don't have computer skills, find someone who can help you with this. These sites don't charge much to print and send you the cards.

Example of information to put on a Calling Card:

Put Your Name
Types of Skills
• Driver's License
• Lawn and Garden Labourer
• Stockperson (Grocery Store)
• Light Duty Cleaner
• Food Handling Certificate
• Work Safety Certificate
• Customer Service Experience
• Computer Skills
Contact Information: Cell: 250-123-4567 and
Email: jobseeker@nota.com

You can leave calling cards with anyone you talk to about your job search. They have your card and pass on your contact information to others. You never know when you might meet someone with a job lead for you!

What will you put on your calling card?

_____

_____

_____

_____

_____

MINI TIP

Those pictures you take on your smartphone describe your journey. Take photos of things you are interested in and proud of. Save them on a USB flash drive. They might become valuable things to talk about at a networking event. Maybe a picture comes in handy to prove a skill at a job interview. What photo do you have that you would be proud to share with others?

TIP №36

The Phone Camera and Job Search

Sometimes, a picture tells a better story about what you can do than words. If you have a smartphone, you have a camera, a valuable tool for your job search.

Use your smartphone to record a picture story of achievements. Take before, during, and after photos of your hobbies and jobs. Photos are proof that you can do the things you say you can do on your resume. You can use the photo in a job interview to help explain your skills and abilities. Here are examples of jobs where a photo would show your work.

- **Car Detailer**—before and after pictures of cars you cleaned.
- **Cook/Baker**—pictures of meals and desserts you have made.
- **Yard clean-up/Gardener**—show how you transformed someone's yard.
- **Hairstylist/Make-up artist**—the skills and creative talent you have.
- **Construction helper**—pictures of the tasks, duties, and tools you used on the job site.

Remember, ask permission before you take photos at work.

Explain that they are for your portfolio. Most employers will permit you to take photos, or they will tell you what you can and can't take pictures of.

Write down some other types of hobbies or jobs that would be good to have a picture of for your portfolio.

_____

_____

_____

_____

_____

Pictures tell a story about your work in a way that words can't. Print off photos for your portfolio. Save pictures online for a digital portfolio. Use a USB flash drive or find an internet site to create a digital portfolio.

What pictures do you already have that show your work?

_____

_____

_____

_____

_____

MINI TIP

Smartphones are great tools to help you stay connected. b Having good cell phone boundaries is also valuable. Remember, employers do not want employees on their phones all the time. Find out the rules at your job. Leave your phone on silent or off. That goes for other electronic devices like watches and digital music players. Use breaks to catch up on emails or texts.

THE INTERVIEW

The following tips are about getting prepared for the job interview.

- Be organized and business-like.
- Take care of last-minute details.
- Be prepared to talk about yourself.
- Understand the importance of the interview.

You have made it to the most critical part of the job search. Call on your support system to help you prepare for the interview. Don't leave anything to chance.

TIP №37
Research the Company

Learn about what the companies do that you are interested in working for. If you don't know what the company does, it will be hard to do the job interview. Employers want to know that you know who they are and what they do. They will ask you why you want to work for them.

Do your research. Make notes in your job search journal.

Things to know about the company:
- Name(s) of the owner(s) or CEO (chief executive officer).
- Whether the business is a private company or a not-for-profit business.
- The education or training they want employees to have.
- The products or services they sell.
- Types of jobs they have.
- If there is more than one business address, find out where the stores, offices, or job sites are.
- The charities the company supports (if they do).
- Their community involvement.
- Mission statement (why they exist).
- Vision (where they are going in the future).
- Principles and values (how they do business).

Most companies have a website and social media. Business owners want to know why you want to work for them. Be able to talk about what you learned about the company and how that information helped you decide you wanted to work there.

What companies are you going to research first?

_____

_____

_____

_____

_____

MINI TIP

Many companies like to give back to their communities. If a company supports a charity, make sure you research that charity too. It tells you more about what the company believes in and cares about. You can talk about their charity work in the job interview if it seems like a good thing to do at the time.

TIP №38
Know Your Community

Know about the town or city you live in. Employers prefer to hire staff that can answer questions that customers have. You may be serving tourists or people passing through town.

When we have a small circle of friends and family, we might only learn about what our group talks about. The information is second-hand, could be wrong, and maybe gossip. It is up to us to learn about your community firsthand through our own experience.

Don't Rely on Social Media To Learn About Your Community
Some social media sites have accurate information, and others don't. It is getting harder and harder to tell them apart! Be aware of the difference. Social media has become a way for people to attack each other. Be sure the information you are reading and passing is fact and not fake.

Research the Community
The best way to learn about your community is to experience it yourself. Get curious about where you live. Read the local news-papers. Pay attention to local news and current events. Travel around town and check out businesses. Talk to people who work in restaurants and stores.

Jobs in restaurants and pubs, hotels, and motels serve tourists. People who work at gas stations meet tourists. Tourists also shop in grocery stores and retail stores. If you work in customer service, expect to be asked questions about your town. Be able to answer them.

Things to Know About Your Community:
- Restaurants—their location, type of food, and a bit about the type of place (fast food, pizza, family restaurant, fine dining, or neighbourhood pub).
- Retail stores—where to buy clothes, camping supplies, snacks, and souvenirs.
- Indigenous knowledge—name(s) of local Indigenous communities and the unceded territory your community is on.
- Tourist attractions like historical sites and museums—where they are, a bit about them, their hours.
- Outdoor public places—for walking, hiking, swimming, golfing, and other sports.
- Hotels, motels, and campsites—where they are and a bit about them.
- Community and cultural events—celebrations, fairs, festivals, and tournaments.
- Grocery stores—where they are and their hours.
- Medical clinics and pharmacies—where they are and their hours.
- Emergency resources—ambulance, fire, hospital, and police department.
- Types of industry—company names and what they do.

If you are targeting a job that doesn't serve the direct public, it is still valuable that you know your community. People you talk to on the phone will want to know where you live.

Employers want to hire people who care about their community. One way to show you care is to know your community.

Be able to talk to customers and give them information and directions around town.

Keep information about your community in your job search journal.

What do you know about your community that a tourist would want to know?

_____

_____

_____

_____

_____

_____

MINI TIP

A side bonus for knowing your community is the opportunities that come your way. You will increase your network and will also be aware of changes when they happen that might lead to new job opportunities.

TIP №39
Arrive in a Clean Car

This tip is as important as personal grooming and hygiene! Remember, first impressions count the most!

You got the job interview! The hard work you have put in has paid off. Nervous and excited, you are preparing yourself for the interview.

Imagine the story below.
You arrive in the parking lot. There is a spot to park right in front of the business. You are thinking...

It's my lucky day! Have I covered all my bases? Hmm... checklist.
☐ Resume/cover letter/job posting.
☐ Portfolio/note paper/pen.
☐ Dressed for success.
☐ Researched the company.
☐ Practiced my interview questions.
☐ Clean teeth and fresh breath.
☐ Arrived ten minutes before.
☐ Do some deep breathing.
I am ready to own this interview!

Then you look up and see with horror two people walking out the door of the building your interview is in.

You ask yourself, "Is that the interviewer walking the last person out to their car? On no! He sees me! He's coming over! My jeep is filthy from last weekend's four-wheeling."

You jump out and turn around. "Is that the 'f' word written in the dirt on the back of the jeep? I can't believe a coffee cup rolled out when I reached for my portfolio. It looks like a garbage dump back there. Where did all that junk come from?"

You realize it too late, "Oh no! I should have cleaned my car!"

A Case of Self-Sabotage!

Your vehicle is part of your image. You don't need an expensive new car to impress an employer, but you do need to arrive in a clean vehicle.

A dirty vehicle says things about your values. It shows how you care for your belongings. If an employer sees that you don't care about your car, they will wonder if you will care about their business. One employer told me he tries to find an opportunity to see a job seeker's car. He said he would never hire a person with a dirty car. A clean vehicle will impress an employer.

If you are borrowing a vehicle, the same advice applies. Clean the car before showing up for the interview. Don't make excuses about the dirty car. Blaming others shows you pass off your bad choices by putting them on others.

Remember

A potential employer considers everything about you before deciding to trust you.

If you have a car, what needs to be done to clean it before interview day?

_____

_____

_____

_____

MINI TIP

Excuses don't work in almost any situation. Only something that happens unexpectedly may be a time you can have an excuse. So, if you are walking or biking to the interview, give yourself enough time. You want time to fix your hair and straighten your clothes. If it is a rainy day, dry yourself off. If it is a hot day, you may need to drink water and freshen up. You want to walk into the interview looking ready for success.

TIP №40
EAT before the Interview

Have something to eat, like a piece of toast or a snack, before the job interview. Eat something so you don't get lightheaded due to low blood sugar. Also, your stomach won't rumble through the interview. You have enough to focus on without feeling embarrassed about your noisy stomach.

Job interviews can be a stressful time. It can be hard to eat on the day of the interview. Still, it is wise to eat something. If your interview is close to breakfast or lunchtime, have a light meal that won't make you feel too full and uncomfortable.

If your interview is mid-morning or mid-afternoon, have a snack before you leave home. If you have a long drive, take snacks in the car.

Snacks to consider:
- Toast and peanut butter.
- Banana.
- Muffin.
- Granola bar.
- Cheese and crackers.
- Wrap with veggies and cheese.
- Sandwich of your choice. (Try to avoid garlic)

Remember
Eat before an interview. You will focus on your interview and not a growling stomach.

What will you eat before your interview?

_____

_____

_____

_____

_____

MINI TIP

Carrying a bottle of water with you is a health and self-care habit. Take one to your job interview. It is hard to focus when you are thirsty. It is hard to talk with a dry mouth. Employers appreciate healthy people and will not have a problem with a water bottle on the table. Just sip it quietly if you need to.

TIP Nº41
Bring These Items to the Job Interview

One of the best ways to impress an employer is to be organized and prepared. It shows you are ready for anything that comes your way.

Bring the items below with you to the interview.

Your Resume and Cover Letter

Bring a copy of the same resume and cover letter (if you used a cover letter) to the interview. Interviews are stressful, and you can forget things. When you have your resume, you can get back on track because your work experience, skills, and abilities are in front of you.

Some interviewers might ask you to walk them through your resume. They want you to explain everything on the resume. You will need your resume for that.

Interviewers might misplace their copy of your resume. It happened to me when I was co-interviewing at a place I worked. It was so great that the person we were interviewing had their copy. We photocopied it and got on with the interview. We greatly appreciated that the person had a copy with her. She also got the job!

The Job Posting

Bring the job posting with you. It is as important as your resume. It can help you remember details about the company. The posting describes what the employer wants and makes it easier to relate your skills and experiences.

A Note Pad and Pen

If the interviewer gives you any information, you can take notes. This way, you don't have to rely on your memory if you feel stressed.

Your Career Portfolio

Bring this with you to the interview. You may get an opportunity to share your portfolio.

Your Personal Information

Make sure you have your personal information with you. Some people get hired right after the interview.

- Your correct address.
- Bank information. (Companies often choose to pay employees by direct deposit.)
- Social Insurance Number.
- Emergency contact person and number.

Remember

Don't share your social insurance number or banking information unless you are offered the job and are filling out the employee payroll forms.

What do you need to collect for the interview?

_____

_____

_____

_____

MINI TIP

You can say yes to a glass of water but say no thank-you to any other drinks or snacks offered while interviewing. If it is a lunch interview, choose a food off the menu that is easy to eat. No messy giant sandwich, burger, or spaghetti! Also, to show good manners, wait until the interviewer orders so you can see how much their food costs and order something at the same price or less. Do not order alcohol.

TIP №42
Answering Behavior Questions

In a job interview, we need to remember past events and what we did during them. They are explained like a story. These stories need to fit the questions that are asked. They must be examples of our past experiences or what we would do in a situation. And they need to be short and to the point. The employer wants to know how we deal with things.

Behaviour interview questions ask you to explain what you have done or would do in a workplace situation. They are asked by interviewers to learn about the following:

- Your experience.
- If you can think through a problem.
- How you handle yourself at work.

It is best to prepare for these questions. Some employers will give out the interview questions ahead of time. If not, you can prepare using the **Common Interview Questions** in the Example section.

Prepare your answers before the interview. Use examples that describe the skills and abilities the employer is asking about. When you don't have work-related experience, ask the interviewer if you can use an example from school, sports, volunteer work, travel, or other situations. The interviewer wants to hear you describe yourself in action. They are looking for your ability to think, react to events, and how you communicate.

Confidentiality

Keep confidentiality in the examples you use. Do not use the names of the people or places in your examples. Use words like co-worker or team, supervisor, manager, owner, or employer. If using school examples, say friend, classmate, teacher, or coach. Say the type of place, like a bakery, grocery store or bank. Not the name.

Answering behavioural questions is not as difficult as it sounds. With planning and using the S.T.A.R. Method, you will be good at answering this type of interview question. The S.T.A.R. Method guides you through the process of explaining your actions.

S.T.A.R. Method for Interviews

STAR is an <u>acronym</u> for a method to answer behavioural questions.

<u>Acronym</u>—**an abbreviation formed from the first letters of other words and pronounced as a word.**

S situation
T tasks
A action
R results

Here is how to set up an answer.

Situation:

Think of something that has happened that will fit the question. Use an example that had a good ending for you. If you don't have something from work, ask the interviewer if you can use an example from your life. Make sure your example is close to what the interviewer is asking. Tell the story as clearly and short as you can.

Task:

Describe what you were responsible for in that situation. The tasks or duties that were part of your job. Make sure to mention any parts that you faced that were difficult.

Action:

Actions are the parts where you describe what you did. Explain how things went using examples of what you needed to do. Talk about problem-solving, communication, quick thinking, teamwork, and how you helped.

Results:

Results are where you get to tell them how things ended. Talk about the positive results of your actions. Explain what might have happened if you hadn't taken the action you did. Describe how the situation might have negatively impacted the business or customer.

The Five Helpers for the S.T.A.R. Method.
Describe
- **Who** was involved.
- **What** the situation is about.
- **Where** it happened.
- **When** it happened.
- **How** it ended.

Let the **Four Ws & H** guide your answers. Prepare some examples, follow the steps, and stay on the topic. Be ready to answer extra questions. Smile and breathe. You will do well.

Common Mistakes Answering S.T.A.R. Questions

Not Answering the Question

If an interviewer asks you a question you don't have an answer, tell them. Be honest. Avoid trying to make something up.

Of course, you still must answer the question. Ask if you can talk about what you would do if you had been in that situation. Think through how you would handle it from start to finish. Use the **S.T.A. R. Method** to guide you.

Not Being Prepared

It is so important to prepare. It is hard coming up with a story on the spot. When people do this, they become nervous, talk too much, and give too much detail. Then, the interviewer is stuck listening to you ramble on and on.

Doing your homework ahead of time means you have some examples prepared. They will also be short and to the point. Try to prepare three to five examples with the skills and abilities the hiring manager might look for. Use the **Tips** on Hands-on and People skills for help.

Prepare examples, but there is no need to memorize them word for word. You do not want to sound fake. Read over your stories before you go in for your interview and focus on the Four Ws & H. Tell things in order. Relax and smile.

Using an Example That Was Not a Success

If asked to describe a time when you wished you handled things differently next time, do not tell a story where you failed and learned nothing. Use an example with lessons you learned.

Using the Wrong Example

Do not use an example that does not answer the question. The interviewer might think you are not listening, are unprepared, or do not have the skills they want. Check with the interview to see if you are on the right track with your example. If you are unsure of the question, ask for clarification. If you do not have an answer, tell the interviewer that. Ask if you can answer a different question.

Using an Example Where You Were Not Qualified to do What You Did in the Situation

Avoid an example where you acted outside of your role at work. If you should have gone to a supervisor but acted instead, you show them you are a risk to hire.

Stay Away from Bragging

Avoid telling a story where you are the only employee doing anything right. No one is perfect. If your co-workers helped, include them in the story. Value your co-workers. Impress the employer with your teamwork values.

Prepare for these questions. Start writing down examples from your experience. You have them! Everyone does. Put the details in point form under the **S.T.A.R.** headings. Decide what questions your example fits under.

See Common Interview Questions in the Example section.

Aptitude Tests

Some businesses ask job seekers to take an aptitude test for the interview process. The employer wants to see if they have the basic skills and abilities that the job requires. Most employers will tell the job seekers beforehand if testing is part of the interview.

Aptitude tests may include things like:
- Typing tests to measure ability and speed.
- Computer tests to measure skills and ability.

- Math skills for the job required.
- Grammar and spelling knowledge.
- Reading comprehension.
- Mechanical reasoning.
- Behavioural questions.

Aptitude tests are often online and timed by a clock. They may be multiple-choice, true and false, or short answers. If you are applying for a job that requires specific hands-on skills, you will demonstrate those skills.

Never let aptitude tests stop you. The first time you do an aptitude test, it will feel hard. A timed test can be stressful. The test questions are unknown. Sometimes, practice tests are online. The best you can do is look at the skills required in the job posting. Practice what you can, like typing, if that is part of the job. You got this!

Aptitude Tests are a new experience for some. Give it your best try. Like anything else, it gets easier the more you do it.

Remember

Keep your interview answers in your job search portfolio for future interviews. Edit them to match the job you are applying for.

What example will describe a time when you made a difference at school, work, or a volunteer situation?

_____

_____

_____

_____

_____

MINI TIP

Self-reflection is a valuable tool for personal success. Self-reflection means taking a few minutes at the end of the day to think about events and how you handled them. Think about the decisions you made and the actions you took. Ask yourself if you would change anything about how you acted or reacted. Self-reflection helps people learn from their mistakes and gives them the power to make better decisions. Writing in a journal even increases the value of self-reflection.

TIP №43
Employers Need
to Trust YOU

No one opens the door to their home and welcomes a stranger in. We do not let just anyone in our life. Do we call a stranger a friend? What do we need before we trust someone enough to invite them into our home? When are we ready to trust them with our things? Trust takes time.

It is easy for an employer to measure hands-on skills. They can do this by watching someone work. Some employees will ask someone they think they will hire to show them their hands-on skills.

It is much more difficult for an employer to know if the person will care about the job. Show up every day for work and do their best. A bad employee can have a very negative and long-lasting impact on a business. They may even ruin the reputation.

Trust and Risk
Employers know they cannot run a business without good employees. Hiring employees is challenging. They hope they hire someone trustworthy, responsible, loyal, and dedicated. During the interview process, the employer decides if they want to take a chance on you. After that, they need to trust.

When hired, an employer decides to trust you with their business. Their business is how they look after their family. Their company is how they make money. Any new employee could pose a risk.

Employees work with products, money, and supplies. You will provide customer service. You will learn private things about how the business works. It is up to you to show the employer that you understand that they must put a lot of trust in you.

Be the employee that you would trust. Keep your word. Be honest, helpful, supportive, and dedicated to your job while you are there. Your future depends on what you do every day. Be that amazing person that people trust and admire.

What does trust mean to you?

_____

_____

_____

_____

_____

_____

_____

MINI TIP

Show you care by being the best you can be. If you are going to be successful, then you must be trustworthy, responsible, loyal, and dedicated. It does not matter what type of work you are doing or whether you will stay with your current job. Treat each job like it's a privilege to work there and take 100% responsibility for your work.

TIP №44
The Power of the Thank-you Card

Being grateful and expressing gratitude is a beautiful way to be.

Thank-you cards are a part of the job search. They are a way to show that you are grateful for the support you received. Give every person who takes time out of their busy day to help you a thank-you card. Tell them why you are thanking them.

Samples of what you might write in a thank-you card.

For an Informational Interview
Dear Ms. Smith
Thank you for taking the time out of your busy day to meet with me. I appreciated the chance to ask you about working in a grocery store. Now I know what the tasks and duties are. Talking with you confirmed that working as a stockperson would be an excellent opportunity for me.
Sincerely, (sign your name)

Job Interview
Dear Mr. Jones
(if there is more than one interviewer, list them by name).
Thank you for taking the time to interview me today. I appreciated the chance to meet you and learn about opportunities for employees. The interview confirmed that working for The

Grocery Company would be an excellent fit and opportunity. I am very interested in the stock person job.
Sincerely, (sign your name)

Remember
The people we do informational or job interviews with become part of our network. Receiving a thank-you card from you shows them:
• You have manners.
• You are interested in the type of work.
• You are grateful for their time.
• You are serious about employment.

Even if the employer decides not to hire you, the card you give them might sit on their desk for a bit. When other opportunities come up, if someone they know is looking for an employee, they will remember you because you took the extra step. The card is a reminder you are out there!

Giving a thank you card shows your excellent people skills.

Can you think of other ways people can help you with your job search?

_____

_____

_____

_____

_____

_____

MINI TIP

Write down the first and last names of everyone you meet. Put a short note beside their name with details about them, where you met, and what happened. Keep this information in your job search journal. You never know when you might come across them again. They will be very impressed with you!

EMPLOYMENT

You got the job. Congratulations!

The following tips will help you through your first weeks.

- Listen and learn.
- Ask questions.
- Write down what you learned.
- Don't give up.

Learning your new job is your responsibility. Be prepared every day.

TIP №45
Carry a Small Notebook and Pen

When we start a new job, the first few days will feel confusing and overwhelming. We are beginning a brand-new experience. There is a lot to learn. It helps if we remember that every employee has had a first day. They have felt much of what we are feeling.

It is up to you to look after what you need to be successful. Let's put some support in place for the first few weeks in your new job. The more prepared you are, the easier your first few weeks will be.

Training Days

The first few weeks of work focus on training. A supervisor or employee will teach you the job tasks and duties. You must listen to them carefully and ask lots of questions. Learn how to do the job.

Not all employees may be good at training new staff. Trainers may not know how much you need to learn. Tell them when you don't understand something. Do not pretend to understand. Ask questions.

Small Notebook

Carry a small notebook and pen with you at work. Pull it out when given instructions and write down important details. Use this tool to remember the information you learn every day.

First-day information to write down:
- Names of employees you meet and their jobs.
- Start times and end times.
- Parking rules.
- Break times and lunchroom rules.
- Job tasks and duties.
- How to fill out your timesheet.
- Name of your direct supervisor.
- First aid and safety rules.

Don't Rely on Your Memory

Your training days will be much easier if you keep track of what you are learning. Write down things like how the cash register works or how to use a plan-o-gram for stocking shelves. Your trainer will be impressed that you are taking notes. On your break, record things you have learned during the day. As you start learning, you'll be glad you have your notebook.

When you know your job well, things still come to be remembered. Write them down. Successful people make notes and keep track of their days. They write important things down and never rely on just their memory!

What are some of the things you want to learn in your new job?

_____

_____

_____

_____

_____

_____

MINI TIP

If you have trouble with spelling and this makes you avoid writing things down, buy an erasable pen. This writer has been using them for years!

Please remember that you cannot use an erasable pen on legal documents.

TIP № 46
The Value of Questions

Wise people know the value of questions. They are always curious and know there is so much more to learn. They know that they can learn something new from everyone they meet.

This tip is one that you need to remember. Some people feel awkward or shy if they don't understand something. They think questions are a sign of weakness. Questions are not a sign of weakness. Ask questions! Questions helped you through the job search, during the job interview, and getting hired. Questions will make sure you keep your job.

Why are questions so important when you are training? If you don't ask questions, the trainer will think you understand. If you don't, how will you learn to do the work? If you are confused by instructions, you will have to get help or make mistakes that could cost money. Use every chance to ask questions during training.

Learning a New Job (the Learning Process)

First day on the job:
"I don't know what I am supposed to do for my job."

The expert on the job:
"I don't even have to think about how to do my job anymore; I just know it all."

Check out the Learning Process in the Example section.

The First Day on the Job

You will know little about the workplace. You will learn where to park and what it looks like inside the building. You are at the very start of the learning process.

There are so many things to learn. There may be new words, procedures, equipment, software, and people. At this point, you don't even know what you need to learn. Someone will show you around and teach you the basics.

Onboarding

The first day is what is called onboarding. You are:

- Introduced to the other employees.
- Given a desk or workstation.
- Shown the staff room, locker, lunchroom, and washrooms.
- Told when breaks are.
- Given a safety tour and shown the first aid station.
- Told where you can park if you drive.
- Handed a uniform, if required.
- Given employee tax forms to fill out.
- Given a policy manual or employee training manual.
- Assigned a work schedule.
- Introduced to your direct supervisor.

There is lots of information to learn, and you may forget things. Some things may not make sense until you start to do them. Now is the time to start asking questions. And write down the answers in your notebook!

Things Get Easier

After a few weeks on the job, things will start to get easier. You are now understanding how things work.

Every new day will bring learning. You need to make sure you continue to ask questions. Questions prevent confusion. Do not pretend to understand! It will only cause problems later when you try to do the job. Always keep your small pad and pen with you. Write down the answers to your questions.

As you move through the learning process, you become skilled. At some point, you may be the person a new employee can go to for support. That is when it is time to give back by being helpful to others. Never forget your first few weeks and how they felt!

Who has helped you at work or in school?

_____

_____

_____

_____

_____

MINI TIP

Learning a new job takes time. It gets easier every week. It can be a good idea to check in with your trainer or employer and ask them how you are doing. That way, you can work on the areas that need more attention. Employers have what is called a probation period that they might use to decide if an employee is going to work out. The probation period is for learning the job. Check out the probation period that your new employer has.

TIP №47
When to Leave a Job

You got the job! It is so exciting to start your job. Everything is new. There is so much to take in at the beginning. You are busy training and getting to know your co-workers and the business.

At some point down the road, you may think that this is not your forever job.

Months or years into the job, you may want to do something different. Maybe the job is not what you thought it was. It's not a match for your interests now. Changing jobs is part of the career process. Change jobs if you are unhappy. Your career is your responsibility. Do what makes you feel happy.

Do not quit your job until you find a new one. It is best for your financial health. Stay employed while you do your job search. You need money to pay your bills. Never miss a paycheck while looking for work because you quit before you had another job.

It is easier to find work when you are employed. Employers like to hire people who are already working. They have employers who value them. Also, you will find a job easier than someone who has quit and started looking. Why? Remember networking? You are out of the house and around people every day.

If you have a toxic workplace, try not to walk out on the job. Follow the advice above and start a job search right away. You will get better references from your current employer if you give them proper notice when you find a new job.

If you are at risk of injury, that is a different situation. There are circumstances where quitting is the best choice. Talk to someone you trust about the incident(s) if you want feedback.

If you leave a long-term job because you are frustrated, remember confidentiality. Find someone you trust to talk to. Don't share with anyone else. This is an emotional and sensitive time where gossip might happen if you share too much. Even supportive and well-meaning family members might talk. They might feel a need to share your struggles with their close friends. This is how gossip starts.

Changing Jobs While Working:
- Your mentor is the person you can talk to about this.
- In your cover letter, ask to keep your job application confidential until an offer of a job or references is required.
- Stay focused and positive at work. Do your best.
- Give proper notice to your current employer. Give them time to start the hiring process for your replacement.
- Do not say negative things about your previous employer to anyone.

Remember

You have a right to feel happy and supported in your workplace. Sometimes, a job doesn't start that way. Sometimes, the job changes and isn't right for you anymore. You have the right to move on. Do it with kindness and confidence. Go and find your next employment adventure.

What would make you decide to move on from a job?

_____

_____

_____

_____

_____

_____

MINI TIP

You are working now. Start a savings account and put some money aside every payday. You can start small. It adds up. Take some money management courses. Start a budget. Save for the future.

Budget some of your money to keep up your image. Buy new clothes and shoes. You may be comfortable at your current job and can be casual about how you look and present yourself. A new job search requires a refresh of your look. What will you buy soon?

EXTRA ADVICE

The following tips are about extras we can be doing for personal development.

- Create a vision of our future to work toward.
- Act like a boss.
- Read more.
- Stay focused on the positive.

Set goals and enjoy the benefits of achieving them. Live in the moment. Stay excited about the future.

TIP №48
The Power of Vision Boards

Visualization: able to see a picture of something in your mind.

Creating a vision board is a powerful exercise that helps with goal setting and helps keep you looking toward your future. It is a fun and artistic way to stay focused on the future.

Vision boards are a piece of artwork. It is a poster that has pictures and words on it. Many successful people do vision boards often. They use visualization to create a picture poster of the life they want so they stay on track. They put that poster somewhere so they can look at it every day.

Vision Boards Help Provide a Clear Picture of What You Want
We might have thoughts like, I want a better life. I wish things were different. They circle about in our heads. This can cause feelings like stress, frustration, and unhappiness. Capture pictures and words on a poster of the life you want. The vision board keeps your mind focused in a positive direction. No matter what happens during your day, your vision board reminds you where you want to be.

Take some time to visualize what your 'better life' looks like. Don't hold back. Then, create a vision board by clipping pictures and words from magazines that represent specific details of your life. Try this fun exercise. It does help with focus.

What you will need:
- 24 x 36-inch poster board.
- Coloured paper (optional).
- Magazines to cut up.
- Glue.
- Scissors.
- Felt markers and crayons.
- Optional: glitter, paint, treasures to glue on, and maybe a picture of you.

There are no rules on how to approach the design of the vision board. Look through magazines and find pictures and words that describe your best life. Draw pictures. Use the supplies to create a collage of what you want your ideal life to look like.

Design the life you want. Include things like:
- New car.
- New home.
- New friendships.
- Improvements in your friendships.
- Fitness and health.
- Financial freedom.
- Travel.
- Vacation.
- Love.
- Career.

You can add to your vision board as your hopes and dreams evolve. Do a vision board regularly as you build your life. Put them where you can see them every day.

See the vision board steps in the Example section.

A Bit About Motivation

When people know their own **Why** for doing something, they stay on track and refuse to quit. Vision boards are a place to collect your **whys** and display them. Every day, you are reminded of the reason you are working hard. It is one of the best motivations for success. People put their vision boards on a wall they look at every day to remind them of the future they want. Then, they get busy and make it happen.

Once you dream it, believe it is possible. Your brain works behind the scenes (at both a conscious and subconscious level). You start to notice opportunities to act on.

Save your vision boards. Look back at them. See what was on your vision boards that is now in your life!

Vision boards are part of positive thinking. They remind you to start each day with a positive attitude and stay energized to meet the tasks and challenges of everyday life. Many of those challenges will take you forward to the life you want.

What will you put on your first vision board?

_____

_____

_____

_____

MINI TIP

Self-care includes art and play. Make time for healthy fun. Get out in nature. Join a local club that interests you. Pay attention to your creative side. Everyone has one. Try different things until you find one that makes you feel alive. What type of art would you like to try?

TIP №49
Career Planning

We have a company to run. We are the boss of that business. Our career is our company. It is our job to grow and change so our company can. Our business (career) looks after us.

Act like a boss. Believe in yourself. Commit to doing what it takes to have a successful career. Successful people have focus, drive, and work hard. Take charge and be the boss of your career. Do not wait for someone else to tell you what to do.

These are habits that successful people have.

Successful people have the following healthy habits:
- Get up early.
- Eat healthy food.
- Exercise.
- Go to bed early.

Successful people do things differently.

They:
- Arrive early to places they need to be.
- Pay attention to their image.
- Dress for success.
- Manage conflict and are fair.
- Keep their word.
- Accept responsibility and don't blame others.
- Focus on what needs to be done and do it.

- Listen to others.
- Are flexible and cooperative.
- Are creative.
- Gather successful people around them.
- Help others and give back to the community.
- Invest time and resources in improving themselves.
- Think of possibilities and get excited about change.
- Make time for family, friends, and fun.

Plan to be successful. It doesn't matter when or where you are starting in life. Do what it takes to achieve your goals. You have the power to take charge and grow your career.

What is the first thing you, as a boss, will do to change your life?

_____

_____

_____

_____

_____

MINI TIP

There are books, podcasts, videos, and websites by successful people. Study them as much as you can. Choose them over movies, shows, and gaming. You will find that the secret to success is a well-worn trail that anyone can follow. When will you start studying ways to become successful?

TIP №50
Read More

Thank you for reading this book. You wouldn't have made it to the end if you didn't choose to. And life is all about choice.

I wanted to share what I learned from twenty years as a job coach. The result is this book. The job seekers who have sat with me in my office or attended my workshops gave me their trust. They shared their struggles and successes. We learned from each other. We had fun.

My final tip for you is one of my most important messages. Please start reading. Reading is a priceless gift. Learn how. Practice. Read often. Share your reading with others. Just keep reading!

Read for fun. It doesn't matter what you read. Find out what you like to read, then do it every day. There are so many choices! Comic books, magazines, fiction novels, biographies, self-help, motivation, and textbooks all give you the same benefit. They exercise your mind and increase your reading skills. There is so much out there to learn.

Ask for Support
It is never too late to learn to be a reader. If you are starting to learn to read, find a program through a local community college, learning center, or literacy program. Find a free reading program on your computer or smartphone. These programs teach you how to say new words and the meaning of these words. Ask someone in your support system to help you out. They will. I can guarantee it!

Benefits of Reading:
- Opens windows to the bigger world.
- Helps with learning and imagination.
- Increases self-esteem and confidence.
- Provides free entertainment.
- Is part of self-care and relaxation.
- Can help with feelings of loneliness and isolation.

Set a goal to read two new comics, magazines, or chapters in a book in the next thirty days. Reading doesn't need to cost money. Go to your local library, bookstore, or thrift store. Ask a friend or family member to loan you a book.

What will you start reading first?

_____

_____

_____

_____

_____

MINI TIP

Remember, you choose your life. Stay positive, know your **WHY**, stay motivated, set goals, and work hard. You've got this! What is your next step? Life is yours for the taking.

EXAMPLES SECTION

This section has some examples from the TIPS for extra support.

- Informational Interview Questions
- Jessie and His Driver's License
- Networking Journal Example
- Sample Resume
- Basic Guidelines for Cover Letters
- Cover Letter Worksheet
- Sample Cover Letter
- The Learning Process
- Common Interview Questions
- Vision Board Steps

Informational Interview Questions

The questions below will help you prepare.
Not all questions match each job. For example, a person who works building houses does not sit down most of the day. Pick the best questions for the job and the most important to you. Write the questions out in your job search journal.

Do a practice interview with someone before the informational interview. It will help build your confidence.

Remember, most people want to help. It is a compliment to ask people about their careers.

Informational Interview Questions
Make sure to write down the following information:
- Company Name
- Address
- Contact's Name
- Contact's Job Title
- Date of Interview

Choose the questions you will ask or think of your own.
1. What are the things you do every day at work?
2. What do you like most about your job?
3. What skills do you use in your job?
4. Does the job require standing or sitting most of the day?
5. Are there physical demands like heavy lifting involved with the job?
6. Are there parts of the job that are stressful?

7. When do people work? What are the shifts?
   · Monday–Sunday.
   · Monday–Friday.
   · Mornings.
   · Afternoons.
   · Nights.
8. Is the work:
   · Part-time.
   · Full-time.
   · Seasonal (for example, the job shuts down during winter).
9. Do you work in one place or between different work sites?
10. Do people work from home doing this job?
11. What kind of experience and equipment do employees need to work doing this job?
12. Is it possible to learn the skills by training on the job instead of going to school?
13. What certificates are required for this job?
14. Where do most employees get their certificates or education from?
15. What are some of the challenges (hard things) about the work?
16. Are there going to be jobs like this in the future?

Questions About Pay and Benefits
If you want to ask the questions below, then ask permission. "Do you mind if I ask you a question about wages?"
1. What is the wage for a person starting this career?
2. Are there medical and dental benefits?
3. Is a pension available for workers in this type of career? (Pension: part of a worker's wage that is put in a savings plan and paid to the employee after they retire.)

Do as many informational interviews as you need. They are valuable and will help you make better decisions for your future. Keep your interview notes in your job search journal.

Don't forget to send a thank-you card.

Jessie and the Learner's License

Jessie was almost eighteen years old. He did not have his learner's license. Jessie hadn't even tried. He got around town just fine on his bike. He said he wasn't interested in driving.

Unlike Jessie, most teens can't wait to get their learner's license as soon as they are of age. Jessie's parents had been encouraging him since he turned sixteen. They knew Jessie well and realized that his lack of interest was most likely caused by anxiety. His friends were all getting their licences, and Jessie's parents could tell he wished he had his.

Jessie's parents decided they had two choices: let Jessie avoid getting his license or help him face his fears. Knowing how important a driver's license is for getting a job, they chose to help Jessie by giving him a bit of a push.

A driver's training book was given to Jessie. His parents gave him one month to study. They booked the test time and date with the driver testing office. Jessie was told he had to take the test. His parents checked in with Jessie often to see if he was studying. He said yes.

The learner's test day came, and Jessie wanted more time. He said he wasn't ready; he hadn't studied enough. His parents said no. He would be taking his test that day.

Jessie failed the learner's test. He came out of the office feeling bad. His parents praised him for trying. He completed a step toward his license. That was all that counted. And there was a bonus…

Jessie came out of the office with a printout of all the questions he needed to study. He didn't do as bad as he thought. A new exam date was set right then. Of course, Jessie hoped he could have a break, like a year or two. He got two weeks!

His parents promised to help him out by reviewing questions with him. He would make time to practice tests online. He promised no video games or movies until after he had studied.

Test day came, and Jessie went into the testing office. Just fifteen minutes later, he came flying out of the office. Jessie was smiling and waving his learner's permit! He was so excited and proud! It was a huge accomplishment and time to celebrate.

When they got home, Jessie took off to his room to text his friends. His parents had more plans. They knew anxiety around the driver's license wasn't about tests. It was about driving. The driving school was called immediately, and Jessie was scheduled to be picked up for his first lesson.

Over the pizza dinner, Jessie was told that he had driving lessons the next day. He was not happy! Jessie wanted time to get used to having a learner's license. The truth was, he was very nervous about driving a car. His parents knew that the best thing for Jessie was to continue to move forward, so they pushed him to do so.

Jessie had ten driving lessons. He practiced only once between each lesson. He was supposed to practice every day but refused. He was angry with his parents. Despite not practicing much, he passed his road test on the first try! It turned out that Jessie had a natural ability when it came to driving. His anxiety was hiding that.

Today, Jessie drives in big cities. He has had jobs that required driving big delivery trucks. Jessie is a competent, cautious, and good driver. He would tell you that driving isn't a passion. However, he enjoys the freedom and travel that driving gives him … and the well-paying jobs!

Fear and anxiety did not win. Jessie did!

Networking Journal Example

Record every meeting in your Job Search Journal.

Instructions:
1. Fill in the name of the person you networked with (even family members).
2. Put down where you talked to them.
3. Record the time and date when you talked to them.
4. The name or names of people to contact.
5. Write down what you will do to follow up on the lead.

Met with Mr. Smith at his office on Wharf Street.
Time & Date: Tuesday, May 2
Job: The Grocery Store was looking for a cashier
Contact's Name: Talk to Mr. Jackson, the manager
Follow-up: I dropped off my resume at the Grocery Store on May 4. Talked to Mr. Jackson. He gave me a short interview and said he would call me for an interview next week.
**Remember to send Mr. Smith a thank-you card

Remember:
- It is your journal. You don't have to worry about spelling or printing.
- Print the names, times, and dates and what was said.
- It will help you remember the details!

Sample Resume

Job Seeker
1234 Park St., Somewhere, BC V0Y 0Z0
Telephone: 250-123-1234 Cell: 250-123-4567
Email: job11seeker@notreal.com

OBJECTIVE

Please accept my resume for employment as a **Customer Service Ambassador** at **Get Fit Gym**. I am committed to applying my best effort to be a hard-working member of your employee team. **References are available upon request.**

SUMMARY OF TRAINING AND SKILLS

- **Workplace Safety Certificate**
- **Class 5 BC Driver's License**
- **First Aid Certificate**
- **Safe Food Handling** Certificate
- Janitorial experience
- Computer skills

EMPLOYMENT

2022-2023—Stock Person Best Grocery Store, Somewhere, BC

- Stocked canned food and produce. Directed customers to products and bagged groceries for cashiers.

2020-2021—Light Duty Cleaning Clean for You Co., Somewhere, BC

- Worked as part of a team cleaning grocery stores after hours. Operated industrial floor polisher.

2019-2021—Lawn/Garden Laborer Contracts, Somewhere, BC
- Did summer employment by providing lawn-mowing services to individuals.

2019-2022—Daycare Provider Somewhere, BC
- Responsible for afterschool care and safety of my younger sister.

VOLUNTEERISM
2021-Present—Lawn Mowing Services for Seniors, Somewhere, BC

EDUCATION
2022—Graduate Computer and Art, District Senior Secondary School, Somewhere, BC.

Basic Guidelines for Cover Letters

1. **Address the letter to the person hiring:** use their name and title and double-check for the correct spelling of their name. If you can't find their name, use a formal title like "Hiring Personnel."
2. **Write the one-line job target:** provide the position using the words from the job posting.
3. **Connect yourself to the employer:** if you have been referred to the employer by someone, mention them. For example, Mr. Scott, your sales manager, suggested I send you a resume.
4. **Say where you found the job:** if you are responding to a job posting in a newspaper, include the name and date of the paper. For internet job postings, refer to the website and date.
5. **Keep the letter to one page and use a standard business format (12 font and Calibri, Arial, or Times New Roman font):** leave one line space between paragraphs. Type the letter on good quality 8.5 x 11-inch paper.
6. **Keep the letter focused on the position:** show you have done your homework on the company. Share your excitement about the opportunity.
7. **Keep the letter organized:** use the job posting to guide you.
8. **Thank the employer:** for reading your cover letter and resume. Ask for an interview to discuss your skills and experience in detail.

9. **Proofread, then ask someone else to proofread:** check for mistakes.
10. **Sign your cover letter:** include your contact number below your signature.
11. **Attach your resume to the cover letter and give/send it to the employer:** deliver in person if possible or by fax, e-mail, or mail. Follow all the instructions on how to submit your resume that are stated in the job posting.
12. **Make sure you have enough time for your resume to arrive before the deadline on the job posting:** do not depend on someone else to mail, fax, or deliver your letter.

Cover Letter Worksheet

Name of Business:
Date: (date you are sending the cover letter and resume)

Hiring Person's Name:
Hiring Person's Title:

Dear _____ (Hiring Person's Name)

RE: _____ (Job You are Applying For)

Introduce yourself (1 or 2 short paragraphs)

_____

_____

_____

_____

_____

_____

Tell them what you bring to the job (2 or 3 short paragraphs)

_____

_____

_____

_____

_____

_____

_____

_____

_____

_____

_____

_____

_____

_____

Close with a thank you (2 or 3 sentences)

_____

_____

_____

_____

_____

_____

_____

Sincerely,

Your Name
Contact Number

Sample Cover Letter

August 10, 2023

To: Get Fit Gym
  Mr. Jim Owner
  Manager
  4321 Rest St., Somewhere, BC

Dear Mr. Owner,

RE: Application for Customer Service Ambassador at Get Fit Gym

My name is Job Seeker. Get Fit Gym's job posting on the local job bank website caught my eye. I am seeking an entry-level position where I can contribute my skills and experience from my work with Best Grocery.

I have learned customer service, organizational, and cleaning skills from my prior jobs. It is easy for me to be flexible and move from one duty to another as needed. I take ownership of my work and follow up on tasks until they are done.

In my current employment at Best Grocery, I am responsible for stocking canned goods according to the store's strict plan-o-gram. On the ends of the isles, the plan-o-grams change weekly when different products are featured. The current stock must be put away. New products may require different display set-ups and racks built for the new feature. Attention to detail, speed, and accuracy are required.

For the produce department, the fruits and vegetables must be stocked by type and size. They must be inspected all day and spoiled produce removed. Both jobs require that I memorize product codes and know my fruits and vegetables to make sure I can answer customer questions. Cleaning product displays, emptying garbage, and cleaning up spills are part of the job.

As an employee, I believe excellent customer service includes listening to the customers, answering their questions, and assisting them. I am a dedicated, loyal, and drug-free employee. I show up for work on time, support my co-workers, and participate in any training available through the company.

Thank you for taking the time to review my resume. I look forward to an interview to discuss my skills in detail.

Sincerely,

Job Seeker (sign your name)

Job Seeker
Telephone: 250-123-1234 Cell: 250-123-4567
Email: job11seeker@notreal.com

The Learning Process

Incompetence- the lack of ability to do something successfully or efficiently.
I have never worked in a bakery. I don't know how to make bread.

Competency- the ability to do something successfully and efficiently.
I have worked in the bakery for 3 years. I make the best sourdough bread.

First Level
Unconscious Incompetence—I don't know what I don't know. I don't know what I need to learn or where to start.

This is all new to me. I will have to rely on someone else to help me with everything.

Second Level
Conscious Incompetence—There are things I know about the job. There is still a lot I need to learn. I know that.

I still have lots of questions.

Third Level
Conscious Competence—I am getting good at my job. I still must look things up and ask for support, but only when something unexpected or new comes up.

I am getting confident in my job. I still ask questions when new things come up.

Fourth Level

Unconscious Competence—I don't even think about it now; I do my job. It is even difficult to tell someone what I know because much of what I do I don't even think about anymore. My job is automatic. I am an expert.

I am skilled and competent in the bakery. I have mastered the art of baking. I have created recipes and new ways of doing things.

"I can see how far I have come since I started with the company. Three years ago, I had never worked in a bakery. Now, I am responsible for training all the new staff."

We all get to the place of an expert in the job. It is important to remember how we felt when we were new. Reach out to new employees and give them support.

Common Interview Questions

Here are some basic questions to help you get ready for the job interview. Each interview will be different. You will never know what questions will be asked. It is a good idea to spend time getting ready by preparing your answers to these common questions. Use the job posting as a guide to the questions you might be asked.

Common Questions
1. Tell me about yourself.
2. Tell me about your experience with this type of work.
3. Why do you want to work here?
4. What are your strengths?
5. What is one of your weaknesses?
6. What is one of your areas of challenge?
7. What are your long-term goals?
8. Can you work under pressure?
9. Why did you leave your last job?
10. What are some of your interests or hobbies?
11. Can we check your references?
12. Have you ever been dismissed from a job?
13. Do you prefer to work by yourself or with a team?
14. What have you done toward learning new things in the past few years?
15. Why should I hire you?

Behaviour Questions—How you handled yourself in a situation

16. Tell me about a time when you were in a stressful situation at work. How did you handle it?
17. Give me an example of a time when you used good judgment and logic in solving a problem.
18. Tell me about a time when you had to go above and beyond to get a job done. What would you do next time?
19. Tell me about a time when you had too many things to do and were required to prioritize your tasks. How did you do this?
20. Give me an example of when you had to make a split-second decision. What happened after?
21. What is your typical way of dealing with conflict? Give me an example.
22. Give me an example of when you showed initiative and took the lead. What was the result?
23. Tell me about a recent situation in which you dealt with an upset customer or co-worker. How did things end?
24. Give me an example of when you used your fact-finding skills to solve a problem.
25. Describe a time when you saw something that might be a problem and prevented it from happening.
26. You have read the job description for the position. What training do you need to become a productive employee? What steps are you willing to take toward getting the skills necessary to be good at the job?
27. Do you have any questions?

Sample Questions You Might Ask the Employer

Try to have about two to four questions written down before the interview. There is no set number. It depends on what you need to know. If you don't write the questions down, you might forget them. Make sure the questions were not already answered in the interview.

Do not ask questions that are answered on the employer's website or in any information already given to you by the employer. This would show that you did not prepare for the interview.

In some places, the wages must be in the job posting. If this is not a law where you live, it is best to ask about the rate of pay and medical/dental benefits when you are offered the job. Unless the employer brings it up.

Ask Questions About the Job
1. How does the training program work?
2. What are the day-to-day responsibilities of this job?
3. When is the start date?
4. How many hours a week is this job?
5. Is there any travel required for this job?
6. What computer equipment and software do you use?
7. How will my performance be reviewed?

Use the information in the job posting to guide your answers. Get help preparing for the interview.

Remember, no two interviews will be the same. The interviewer will use their own questions. This list is a tool to help you prepare. You still need to expect the unexpected. Do your homework. Practice. You will ace the interview.

Vision Boards Steps

Here are the basic steps to get you started. You decide what you want to use and what you want on your vision board. It is your work of art!

1. Think about things you would like to do.
2. Think about things you would like to have.
3. Use pencils, pens, crayons, felt markers, glue, and magazines.
4. Use a poster board or a blank sketchbook.
5. Use pictures that show what makes you happy.
6. Use words that make you feel good.
7. Create a picture of your vision.

Take some time every day to look at your vision board. Don't make just one vision board. Make vision boards often as you work on your best life.

The Author's Employment Journey

Everyone starts somewhere. Where you end up is up to you!

I started working and earning money when I was twelve years old. I have shared my job history because it has brought me to where I am today. I have had a lot of help along the way. I chose to go back to school, and I have worked hard.

I believe you can do whatever you choose! Know your why, decide your path, and do what you need to do to follow it.

When I Was a Teen.
1. Babysitter.
2. Swept and washed the hallways in an apartment building.
3. Pinsetter at the local bowling alley.
4. Dishwasher and server in a local restaurant.
5. Inventory worker in the freezer department for a local grocery store.
6. Motel room cleaner.
7. Golf ball cleaner at the local golf course.
8. Dishwasher for tournament banquets at the same golf club.
9. Pro shop attendant: club rental, cashier, and sandwich maker at the same golf club.

After High School

1. Airbrush painter of fishing gear in a manufacturing plant.
2. Customer service in a sewing shop in Australia. (I saved my money to go and live there for a year.)
3. Childcare provider while my children were young.
4. Housecleaner.

At Thirty-Seven, I Went Back to College and then University.

1. Community support worker for a person living with disabilities.
2. Employment counsellor.
3. Registered Vocational Rehabilitation Specialist.
4. Workshop facilitator.
5. Retail and customer service trainer.
6. Human resources policy writer.
7. Community resource center support worker and facilitator.
8. College tutor.
9. College exam invigilator.
10. College teacher's assistant.

Present

Today, I am using a combination of every skill I have learned and used in every job to continue to provide services to clients. I continue to educate myself, and I am excited about the future.

Always Remember

Keep At The Job Search
You have lots to offer the employer and the workplace.

Go After Your Dreams
Be brave. You might be scared. Take the chance. Don't limit yourself. Dream big, and then find a way to make it happen.

Look After Yourself
Be safe. Take care of yourself. Wellness is the number one key to happiness and success.

Be You
Stay true to your values and beliefs. You can do great things and live a life you are proud of.

Be Respectful
Think before doing. Success is always based on your actions. Be kind and think of others.

Take Responsibility
You are responsible for your actions. Clean up after yourself. Fix what needs to be fixed. Say sorry.

Say Yes More
Life is more fun when you say yes. Saying yes can lead to amazing adventures.

Have Fun
Make time for play. Stay in the present and enjoy your journey.

Give Back
Every act of kindness makes a difference.

Thank you for reading my book. I hope you keep it close by while you are on your employment and career journey. Remember to believe in what you will do. Learn something new every day. Change happens, so be ready for change. Stay motivated and look for inspiration. Choose to live your best life!

Janice M Nielsen

ACKNOWLEDGEMENTS

First, I would like to thank my spouse, Patrick, for your support. It takes time to write a book. Much of my free time in the past two years has been spent in front of a computer. I worked, and you took care of things around the house. You went off and did things on your own. When I needed a break, you would whisk me off for some fun. If I was stuck, you would listen with patience and encouragement. I felt supported and loved. All my love and gratitude.

Next, I would like to express my sincere gratitude to J.R. Silver. When I first talked about writing this book, you endorsed the idea. When I didn't start it, you kept asking me when I would get busy writing. When I started, you gave me a timeline. That moved the book along. You listened, read, edited, and gave me valuable feedback. Repeatedly! You helped me navigate out of the weeds every time I paddled into the marsh of self-doubt and got tangled up. Without you, this book would still be a goal without action. You are my mentor and friend!

Thank you to my children, family, and friends. I was busy writing in my spare time when I could have spent it with you. I am grateful for your support and encouragement along the way. I appreciate and love you all!

Thanks to Amber, my publishing specialist, for her support and expertise. I had lots of questions, those new writer questions. You answered them all with patience and care. I learned a lot from you and felt supported.

To FriesenPress and the publishing team that worked on my book, from the manuscript evaluation to the final book, a huge thank you!

To the job seekers that I have served, my gratitude. Each of you taught me so much about courage, strength, and determination. Thank you for your trust, patience, and hard work. It is not easy looking for employment. The reward is worth it.

Printed in the USA
CPSIA information can be obtained
at www.ICGtesting.com
CBHW021152190724
11674CB00002B/179